THE
Wanderer

THE
Wanderer
DION'S STORY

DION
DIMUCCI
WITH
DAVIN
SEAY

BTB
BEECH TREE BOOKS
WILLIAM MORROW
New York

Library of Congress Cataloging-in-Publication Data

Dion, 1939–
The wanderer : Dion's story / Dion DiMucci with Davin Seay.
p. cm.
ISBN 0-688-07841-9
1. Dion, 1939–   . 2. Rock musicians—United States—Biography.
I. Seay, Davin. II. Title.
ML420.D56A3 1988
784.5'4'00924–dc19
[B]   88-19419
CIP
MN

Printed in the United States of America

First Edition

1   2   3   4   5   6   7   8   9   10

BOOK DESIGN BY JAYE ZIMET

BĪB

The word "book" is said to derive from *boka*, or beech.
The beech tree has been the patron tree of writers since ancient times and represents the flowering of literature and knowledge.

To Susan—you're the greatest.
To Jack—I pray I can pass it on.
To Zach—you're the best.

Acknowledgments

To Walt Quinn—thank you for bringing Davin and me together, and for your thoughtfulness

To my daughters, Tane, Lark, and August—the love and inspiration of my life

To my parents, Pat and Fran, my sisters, Joan and Donna, and
my brothers, Tommy and Santos—you're precious to me

To Davin Seay—for your talent, energy, and commitment

To the teachers, mentors, and friends who have encouraged
and supported me along the way: Dick Clark, Dan Mur-
row, Donny Moffet, Bill Whipple, Paul Simon, Mac, Pas-
tor Chuck Smith, Greg Laurie, Steve Van Zandt, Bruce
Springsteen, Paul Shaffer, Bill Tuohy, Kenny Laguna, all
the guys at WCBS-FM Radio, New York, Bill W. and
Lois and all their friends—thanks

—Dion

To Diane—above and beyond the call . . . as usual. All love

—Davin

Contents

Introduction

IT was one of those warm summer nights in the city, when neighbors sit talking on their stoops and lovers take slow walks down the old streets—streets where they grew up and where their kids will grow up. One of those nights where the traffic sounds like a lullaby and the smells of a dozen different kinds of food float by on the breeze. It was June. It was New York City. And it felt like coming home.

In Midtown, there was a line around the block of Radio City Music Hall, a line of people all feeling the same feelings. They'd come from the five boroughs, from Jersey and the Island and Philly, and even out from the Coast. They brought their girlfriends and boyfriends— the ones they'd grown up with, and then married—a little older now, a little wiser, but still looking good. And they brought their kids, jumping up and down on the plush seats, wondering what all the excitement was about. They were all waiting for the lights to go down and the curtain to part. They'd come to hear the old songs.

We go back a long way, me and the people that packed that hall in the summer of 1987. We share a lot of the same memories, good and bad, a lot of the same dreams and disappointments. When I sang, they listened and when they listened, it felt so right. They knew all the words, all the melodies . . . had probably sung them a thousand times in the shower or on the way to work, when the car radio picked up the oldies station. They could tell you the date one record hit the streets or another topped the charts. They could tell you where they were the first time they heard "The Wanderer," do a note-perfect rendition of the doo-wop harmony on "I Wonder Why," or relive the backseat romances sparked by "Where or When." They knew those tunes better than I did, but they still wanted me to sing them, and for the first time in a long time, I did, too.

Sometimes the past can seem like a ball and chain. You know the feeling—you open up the school yearbook or pull out a shoebox of old snapshots and there you are, young and full of yourself and ready to give the world a run for the money. You laugh, partly because the clothes and hairstyles are so out of date and partly because you're hiding the hurt. If you only knew then what you know now. If you only had a second chance.

I guess that's what the Radio City show was all about—a second chance. For a long time I wanted to forget about that kid with the hit records and the high-rolling life-style, the kid everybody'd come to see one more time. He was the ghost of a lot of dreams gone sour, the Mook with the Most who ended up with a whole lot of nothing. A punk with sharp threads and an attitude, he'd done things I wasn't too proud of. I didn't want to take responsibility for who he was and what he meant to a whole lot of people; people who just liked the sound of his voice and the way he combed his hair. For them, Dion was one of their own who made good, a hero in a time when things were simpler and life was like a movie. But that Dion, for me, was a dark stranger consumed by a hundred forms of fear. That kid had almost ended up a dead legend, one more sad show business saga, a poster where a person used to be. For a whole lot of years, the best way I could get by was to deny that guy, to keep him hidden in the shadows of the past, to look ahead but never behind.

It wasn't easy. People kept asking me to sing the old songs, just one more time, and if I couldn't get around it, I'd knock off a verse or two, poking fun at the memories, making them laugh to hide my pain. I was a family man now, with three lovely daughters and a wife whose high tolerance for unacceptable behavior had pulled me through more than once. I'd written a lot of music—a lot of good music—since the old days, and those were the songs I wanted everyone to hear, with words about hope and safety and serenity. And when they listened to those songs, they mostly felt good, too. But there was always that ghost waiting in the wings, waiting for a chance to bring back the glory days.

So when my old friends at WCBS-FM asked me if I wanted to do a show—to do the old songs for old times' sake—I started to give them the old answer: thanks, but no thanks. Then something stopped me. Suddenly, it seemed right; now was the time to make peace with myself, with a kid named Dion who'd once been famous. And foolish. And afraid. I guess what I'm saying is that I had a chance to forgive myself. And I took it.

It was harder than you might think. I wrestled with a

lot of old feelings in the days and weeks before the concert. Those songs, and all they stood for, were a part of a life I'd turned away from a long time ago. To face it all again was painful and a little scary. I didn't want to start living in the past, to find out that people liked me better then than they do now. Maybe it's something every entertainer goes through, but that didn't make it any easier.

One night, just a week or so before the big event, it all came to a head. I was still unsure of myself and why I'd ever agreed to do the one thing I'd resisted for so long. I took a walk, to try to think things through. Did I want to breathe life into something that had died twenty years ago? Was I as nostalgic for glamour and excitement as my fans? Did I still have something to say, as a singer and a songwriter, or were my best tunes behind me? I've recorded lots of albums since the days of my early success, sung in concerts around the world, and written songs that people told me had changed their lives. Why did I want to go back? What was I trying to prove?

I needed the answer, and when it came it was in a still, small voice that wasn't my own. "Hey," the Lord said. "Relax. They want to hear the old songs. It makes them feel good. There's nothing wrong with that, is there, Dion?"

You know something? He was right. As usual. Radio City Music Hall felt good that night. My family was there—Susan and the kids, mom and dad and my sisters, right in the front row. The band was hot and so was the crowd. Cousin Brucie was there. So was Carlo from the Belmonts, hitting notes like he was still on Crotona Avenue and twenty years had never happened. And when we opened up with "That's My Desire," well, the place just came apart. Suddenly, I knew what I was there for.

Because I love to sing. Because people want to hear me sing. And because there's nothing wrong with that. . . .

When it was all over and the people had gone home, I was left alone with my own memories. Not all of them gave me a warm feeling for the good old days. But not all of them made me believe I'd be better off for not having lived through it. It was my life. I owned it and it was no good pretending it happened to someone else. It was time to lay it all out, the good with the bad, to see what kind of sense it made. For me and maybe for others.

We've all asked ourselves the old question: What would I change if I had to do it all again? A lot or a little—we've each got a different answer. What would I change if I had the chance? I guess my answer would be nothing, except that same old need to change everything, to make it fit the way I thought my life should be—the way it was in the movies. I spent too many years trying to fix things—my career, my family, my destiny—and when I couldn't make it right, I got mad. And when that happened, I started tearing things down, hurting others, but mostly just looking for ways to hurt myself. Hey, I'm not a shrink and I'm not a priest. I'm an Italian kid from the Bronx who sings for his supper. What I know, I found out the hard way. So when I finally learned how to accept the way things really are, the good with the bad, it was one lesson that really stuck. If that can happen to me, it can happen to anyone.

I guess that's why I decided it was time to settle accounts with the past—to write this book. If I could sing my songs and make people feel good, maybe I could tell them my story, too, and give them something to take home after the music fades. At least, I hope so.

There's been a lot of thrills and chills in my life,

some fast climbs and dizzying drops. I was lucky to be in the right place at the right time, rocking the cradle of rock and roll, and when I look back at all the wild scenes I've been through and all the once-in-a-lifetime people I've met, sometimes all I can do to keep from crying is to shake my head and smile.

When it comes down to it, this is a story about learning how to accept. About losing everything and finding yourself. Like singing the old songs, a time comes when it's right to remember. Not what I wished might have happened. Not what I wanted to happen. But what really went down. Like I was saying, sometimes all we really need is a second chance. To set the record straight. To say I'm sorry about that or I'm proud about this. A chance to tell the truth.

This is my chance.

CHAPTER 1

Roots and Echoes

WHEN I was growing up, a son of Italy in the heart of the Bronx, I used to see pictures of other kids in magazines or the movies. They'd be surfing in California or pitching hay on a farm somewhere, and even though it seemed exotic and exciting, I felt a little sorry for them. They were part of another world. They didn't know what it was like to grow up Italian, to be a part of the neighborhood, in the middle of the greatest city of them all. I felt special, privileged, like I'd been born under a lucky sign. When you're a kid, life is a story book, starring you. My story took place in a kingdom full of dangers and delights, like no place else in the world.

The center of that kingdom was Crotona Avenue and 187th Street. A lot of my life, and the lives of my friends, unfolded on that corner. Tragedy, comedy, romance, it was all happening, twenty-four hours a day, seven days a week. The street was the place where you took your shots and learned your lessons, where you proved who you were and dreamed about who you wanted to be. It was like a stage—a stage filled with larger than life characters.

My grandfather, Frank, for instance. He died when I was about eight, but I remember him like yesterday—a big man, awesome, with hands like whole prosciuttos and a taste for red wine. I remember my dad telling me about how he used to jump on his old man's back when Frank had too much to drink, trying to hold him down. It was like wrestling a bear, he'd say.

Or Maria, my grandmother on my dad's side. She was very religious, with a kind of stubborn faith that came over with her from the old country, from Bari, right on the heel of Italy's boot. My family talks about Maria to this day, about her beautiful high cheekbones and how much she loved the Lord. I can remember running up the stairs of the building where they lived, and I can remember the look on her face when she answered the door. She'd turn her eyes to heaven and thank Jesus just for the pleasure of seeing me. Then she'd give me a big hug and kiss and drag me inside where there was always food on the table. "Eat," she'd say and fill me up with her good homemade bread and fresh cheese.

She got that cheese right across the street at Joe's Grocery. Joe knew everything: He knew who died, who was pregnant, who was getting married and divorced. You couldn't keep a secret from the guy, which meant that sooner or later everyone in the neighborhood would find out. Joe liked to feed me, too. Funny, but food was a way of showing love and if you weren't hungry, well, it didn't much matter. They'd fill you up anyway. With Joe, you couldn't go into his shop without getting personally involved. Ask for a piece of mortadella on white bread and it was like you'd insulted his sainted mother. "You're

going to ruin my meat with that white bread," he'd shout.
"Let me give you some good Italian bread, just baked
today. That's how you eat mortadella!" And by that time
his wife would be out of the back room with a plate of
peppers and he'd be piling them on the sandwich, too.
You'd never get away from Joe's with anything less than
a deluxe hero, peppered with the latest gossip.

If you took a right out of Joe's and walked down
Crotona Avenue, heading toward the Bronx Zoo, you'd
come up on Crazy Tony's candy store with all the mirrors
out front, the one where we'd stand night after night
combing out dips and watching the girls sashay by. A little farther down was Tally's, the poolhall where the great
Mosconi once ran over a hundred balls. Talk about larger
than life; Mosconi was a beautiful cat, classy, with steel
gray hair and camel hair coats, a hustler in the grand old
tradition and a guy you admired if you were a kid on the
street, looking for someone to be.

Keep going down Crotona Avenue to the main drag,
187th Street, and hang a left. You'll be heading right for
Mount Carmel, the parish cathedral and the hub in the
wheel of my little kingdom. It was big and dark and kind
of spooky inside that church; I can still smell the mustiness
of old hymn books and incense. My dad brought me there
every Sunday for the first eight years of my life, not because he was so pious, but because he liked to listen to the
pipe organ. After the organist died, we never went back.
None of us, that is, except my grandmother Maria.

You couldn't really say that God was a part of my
world. The old folks, the ones who had come over on the
boat, maybe they still knew what it was like to have re-
ligion, to pray and believe they were being heard. Their
God was the one who brought the rain, the grape on the

vine, and the harvest in its time. They had a faith that was tied to the earth and the seasons but in the middle of that city, where only concrete and steel and brownstone brick broke the horizon, the old ways were passing slowly away. It was a new age, in a new country where Frank and Maria and the other old-timers held on to their traditions—of drinking and the church—for dear life.

I never found God in that high arched ceiling, but maybe I wasn't really looking. For me, and for my best friend, Ricky Giuliano, Mount Carmel was just another part of the neighborhood that had been around a long time before we showed up and would be there long after we'd gone. It seems to me, that as a kid, the world was divided into things that were my size and things that were way over my head. God was a million miles away in Mount Carmel, somewhere up above those stained glass windows. The priests and nuns could give you the fear of God, all right, and the guilt that came from not following the rules, but they couldn't breathe life into the words and rituals.

Ricky I've known my whole life—another character. I used to call him "Brainstorm" because Ricky was always cooking, he always had ideas. We liked to hang out the window at my grandmother's house during the religious festivals. The neighborhood would set up a stage, right below her apartment, painted with flowers and really ornate, and they'd get a band and an opera singer and there'd be music all night. From Maria's we had a box seat for it all and during the Feast of Saint Anthony they'd wheel this statue down the middle of Crotona Avenue, with all the elderly ladies in black gowns and rosary beads following behind. The merchants in the neighborhood used to come out and pin money on the statue, and Ricky got to thinking. We should get our own statue, he said, and work Southern Boulevard. I don't remember whether it was Maria or Mr. Giuliano who put a stop to that.

Mr. Giuliano was a part-time voice teacher and when Ricky and I weren't building clubhouses down at the botanical gardens, he'd give me a few singing pointers. Music is something I can't remember ever being without. One of the first things I realized about myself was that I could grab a handful of notes, open my mouth, and take people on a trip. Sitting on the stoop with my friends, the music would flow from something deep and natural inside me and wash over them, and those moments were the closest thing to magic that I can remember. It was like a special power, a gift that had always been there. When I was in the middle of music, I felt like someone. I felt connected.

It helped getting lots of encouragement. My Uncle Lou bought me a hock shop guitar and taught me a few chords. After a while he took me around to Ermondo's, a local hangout, right up Fordham Road across from Bronx Park. He'd get me up on the stage, just a wooden platform at one end of the club, and I'd sing a song and they'd all go crazy over me. Because I was underage, they'd hide me in the kitchen when the law came by to check up on things. I became like a local attraction by the time I was eleven and the customers would put money in the hole of my guitar, especially on Friday night, after payday, when the drinks flowed freely. Sometimes I'd earn twenty, thirty dollars in a night. It was like the statue of Saint Anthony—I was on to something.

I'd take that guitar everywhere—hallways, club-rooms, but mostly the front stoop. Our landlord, Mike, was a stonecutter, the same guy who once carved the steps outside our apartment, where I used to sit and play. He bought the first tape recorder in the neighborhood and once in a while his wife, Adaline, would let me use it. I liked to hear the sound of my own voice on that old reel to reel, but what I liked better was getting all the kids in the neighborhood together who had any bit of talent, from playing accordion to making mouth noises. I'd organize a band and we'd spend hours putting down songs, practicing our chops. It all came so naturally.

The DiMuccis lived at 749 East 183rd Street on the top floor of a two story walk-up. The place had two bedrooms, a bathroom and kitchen, small for a family of five, but we made do. My sisters, Donna and Joanie, lived together in a space that doubled as a living room, with foldout couches for the daytime. My room was the last one, down the long hall of the railroad flat, next to my folks.

The rent on that place was thirty-five dollars a month. It seemed like a lot of money then, and even after I became a success, thirty-five dollars was a way to measure the worth of something. My family was in the millinery business. My mom's dad, Tony, made felt hats, pressing the thick fabric over molds and then passing them on to the women, who'd sew ribbons and hat bands. For a while my Mom did piece work, taking the Sixth Avenue D train into Manhattan every day, where she worked in a sweatshop. We weren't rich, not by any measure, but we always had food on the table and clothes on our backs. We were part of a dream, an American dream of a better life, of peace and plenty, and if that dream didn't quite come true for my folks or for their folks, well, there was always the kids. It was like the future was always just being born in the neighborhood, always trying to find a place of its own. The streets were part delivery room, part funeral parlor and on every corner the new and the old did the same timeless dance.

⤳ The rest of my family—aunts and uncles and second cousins and old ladies from the old country—were spread out all over the Bronx. During the holidays, or for a wedding or funeral, it seemed like they all came over to our place for dinner—two hundred and fifty Italians, all talking at once. They were a handsome gang, my family. My mom's four sisters would always show up with their husbands—big, boisterous guys like Lou, and Uncle John, the neighborhood electrician. There'd be a big pot of spaghetti and lots of laughing and, of course, singing. My grandfather Tony always sat at the head of the table with a jug of wine. He'd pour you a glass depending on how old you were; a little wine and a lot of 7-Up if your chin didn't come up over the table, a little more wine and a little less soda if you weren't wearing short pants. He was a strong man, like Frank, but with a beautiful temperament, and he was the natural head of the clan.

Summers, the family would pool all their money and we'd rent a bungalow up in the Pine Plains or Mahopac in upstate New York. The men would go into the city to work and the women would cook these huge meals while we kids would swim or play in the tall trees. Those were great times; slow and easy and it seemed like the green months would never end, until you'd catch the first whiff of autumn on the wind and your folks would buy you a new pair of jeans and sneakers for school.

I went to P.S. 32 where I fell in love with my third grade teacher, Mrs. Firestone. I took flowers to her house once, only to find out she was married. It broke my heart. I was a good student, especially at math, but quiet and a little shy, I guess. I liked sports, stickball, swimming, and always was one of the first kids chosen on the playground teams. But what I was more interested in was painting fanciful sets for the school play. There were girls I liked, that I tried to get around, but I just didn't know how. I never did really have a steady girlfriend until later, in junior high school at P.S. 45, when I started going with Virginia Petriello.

I fell in love with Virginia, with her thick black hair and sparkling brown eyes. She went to the Catholic school at Mount Carmel and one year they were having a camp fire play and needed someone to play songs for the show. So they kind of borrowed me from the public school and brought me over to sing and strum in this all-girls play. That's where she caught my eye. A few days later I asked Virginia if I could carry her books. I walked her up to 187th Street and invited her into Crazy Tony's for an egg cream.

My heart was pounding as we went into the drug-store and sat down at the counter. I wanted to do every-thing just right, to impress her with my cool. So I ordered two egg creams and tried to pay for them. There I was, juggling her books and my money and these two egg creams and I guess it had to happen. But why me? One of those thick drinks landed right on Virginia's lap. All I could do was stare as it drained off through her lime green dress. Moments like that just never seem to fade.

In a way, I'm constantly being reminded of what it was like to grow up in that neighborhood, at that time. Everywhere you look, you pick up the memories. Movies and TV celebrate the myth of the dago street kid, half

Valentino, half Al Capone. From Fonzie to *The Lords of Flatbush,* I keep seeing the image of that little kingdom, hearing the music and the lingo that made it so special, so exclusive. Hindsight is perfect, I guess, so it doesn't bother me that people remember it all as the Good Old Days. Sometimes it does all seem to have a golden glow. When I was a kid, five or six years old, I had a stride, a way of walking that matched the joy I had for life, for the adventure of being alive. I'd stroll down the streets of the neighborhood shouting out to people I met. It was good to be alive on Crotona Avenue at the dawn of rock 'n' roll.

For me, though, it's not that simple. Life was good then, sure; it was slower and sweeter. But even in our innocence, even as kings in our own realm, we could feel the pull of forces we couldn't control, of scenes from which there was no escape.

CHAPTER 2

The Puppeteer

THE first thing I remember, when I was two or maybe three years old, was taking a ride on my dad's shoulders, hanging on to his curly hair with my head inches from the sky. Together we'd go into the park and just look at the clouds. He'd make shapes out of them and then tell stories about the shapes and from that perch it all seemed so much closer. I felt like I was on top of the world.

Pasquale DiMucci is his name: first-generation American, native New Yorker, jack-of-all-trades, master of none. He's small and strong, built to last and to this day he still swims in the canals down in Miami while the old folks on the shore yell at him to watch out for alligators. He's another larger-than-life character, a strange mix of a guy who, when I was a kid, sometimes seemed like a kid himself.

He never took an aspirin, he likes to say: never been sick a day in his life. He was into health food, healthy living, back when pasta and lots of it was the neigh-

borhood diet. We'd go out to the Botanical Gardens and
he'd climb up a steep hill overlooking the lake and strip
down to his shorts, diving into the water like Johnny
Weissmuller.

He loves nature; he'd pick up leaves and tell me,
"There's a whole galaxy here, Dion. Just look." Nature,
for him, was a kind of God, a benevolent one that provided for his every need. The stars, the sand on the sea-
shore—it was like his world had no limits. And he
couldn't get enough of it.

He tried to pass it on to me—his artistic temperament, his way of looking at life. He tried to get me to
sculpt and paint and find shapes in the clouds and I tried,
even though I was really looking for something else.

I love my dad, loved him even when I didn't want to
be his son. Pasquale is a man totally comfortable, totally
wrapped up, with who he is. And sometimes that didn't
leave a lot of room for anyone else. I never figured out
whether he was ahead of his time or helplessly behind it.
All I knew was that in the neighborhood, in the family,
he wasn't considered just the black sheep. He was a
wash-out, plain and simple.

Part of it was the times, back before the Sixties,
when no one even knew about "alternative life-styles."
They all played by the same rules, and if you didn't play,
you could never win. My dad never had a steady job,
never paid taxes—never made enough money to pay
taxes. Pasquale, the dreamer, was the family's poor rela-
tion and it wasn't long before he became the brunt of
their jokes. He was a babe in the woods when it came to
business, the kind of man other men found it easy to feel
superior to. When they all marched away to the Second
World War, he told stories about how he'd talked his way

out of the draft. During those Mahopac summers, my father would stay with the women at the bungalow while my uncles went to work. You noticed those things, even when you're just a kid.

It was hard to respect a man like that and, for me, respect was everything. Sure, I'd been taught the code on the street, but, in my life, getting respect went way beyond that, way beyond just winning. I started losing all perspective, driven by the need to be looked up to, admired, loved. I loved my old man but when I heard my uncles laughing behind their hands, I never wanted to be like him. Deep inside was the feeling that no one would ever treat me like that, no matter what it took.

That feeling stayed with me through the early years of my singing career. When I got my first big record, it was like I was showing my uncles that they'd better take notice. That they'd better stop laughing now. I saw that people changed when you had some success. My family treated me differently, like I was someone who mattered, not like my father. It wasn't as if I'd really earned their love and admiration, but it wasn't like it really mattered, either. It was a game and I liked being the winner.

Pasquale married Frances, my mom, when he was twenty years old. She'd been engaged to Angelo, a big, strapping, wonderful guy, to hear her tell it, and, as the neighborhood milkman, a real catch. Even my grandmother loved him. But the night he asked her to marry him, Angelo fell asleep at the wheel on his morning run and was killed. To this day, my mom cries whenever talk turns to Angelo and what could have been.

If I'd been Angelo's son, who knows? Maybe I would have lost some of the zest for life, that special feeling I had when I was a kid that everything was going my way, that every day really was an adventure—those same feelings my dad always talked about. And, maybe, if things had been different, I wouldn't have carried such a big load of resentment around for so many years.

But it didn't work out that way. I was Pasquale's son, his first born. I had a fear of my dad, and for the old country ways he had learned from his father. He taught me how to swim by throwing me off a raft in the middle of the lake. But I didn't swim back to the raft. I headed for the shore, to get away from him. As a father, he was impulsive, aggressive. I never knew quite what to expect. As a man, there were parts of him that you just couldn't square, those private places that the real world couldn't touch. He had three kids, a wife, and all that went with them. But more than anything else, he loved his puppets.

Pasquale made $70 a night, when he could, as a puppeteer, hanging on the fringes of the old vaudeville scene, the Catskills, and the gilded movie palaces in Brooklyn and the Bronx. He crafted all his comic heroes and villains in the attic of our house, shaping their faces out of plaster of paris and his own imagination and carefully painting on their expressions of joy, anger, and amazement. They were his own creations, but I always thought they were parts of who he was, too, like clues about where he came from and who he wanted to be.

In one of his skits, a dancer strutted while a puppet pianist and saxophonist played. My dad would sing behind the curtain, a truly unforgettable sound. People would try to discourage him, but he'd sing anyway—old Al Jolson songs out of tune with no sense of rhythm. One thing I had no doubt about: I didn't get my musical talent from Pasquale DiMucci. The way he sang always kind of reminded me of Eddie Fisher.

In another one of his shows, a kid floats away on a balloon until it pops and he falls back to the stage. There was a clown telling jokes, dancing girls, and, sometimes, sword fights. He had a skeleton, Day-Glo painted against a black curtain, that would come out and do a soft-shoe and then, in the middle of the number, fly apart, the bones lying in a heap on the stage, still moving in time to the music. It was a fantasy world, bright and colorful and full of laughter.

After Angelo died, my mother mourned for two years. She was in black the day she met my father. He kind of took her mind off things, took her away from the questions she couldn't answer. He did handstands, told her stories, acted the clown. Pasquale was different, like no one my mother had ever seen before.

Frances DiMucci, my mother, has never had a day in her life when she isn't worrying about something, looking out for someone or taking charge somewhere. If my dad's motto is "stop and smell the roses," hers is "wake up and smell the coffee." She was born to bear responsibility, and the heavier it got, the more long-suffering she got. In most important ways, she held the family together, making hats with her father and making ends meet at home.

Responsibility came naturally for my mom, from when she was a girl and helped to raise all her four younger sisters and three brothers: cooking meals, cleaning up, taking care of everyone. She brought it into her married life, always taking care of business, while my dad was up in the attic making puppets or down in the basement lifting weights. She was a fixer, forever trying to make things right. It's something she passed on to me, that certainty that if I could just control circumstances and conditions, I could make everything add up the way I thought it should. But people never did what I wanted them to do. *I* never did what I wanted me to do. I didn't realize that change had to start inside, with me.

My mother used to take me aside, just the two of us, and tell me that I had to save her from all this, to take her away from a life that hadn't worked out the way she wanted. She was big on appearances, but behind it all she was desperate and she wanted me to be her rescuer. It was another driving reason for me to succeed, because I thought that somehow her happiness, and the survival of the family, depended on having more than enough of everything. I wanted to buy them their freedom.

Money was the one thing my parents argued about all the time, the one thing everyone, including my mother, ridiculed my dad about. She was always on him to find a decent job, and he was always a million miles away, pulling strings on a cloud. She would chew him out in front of the family, with my uncles helping, and it was her feelings toward him, more than anything, I guess, that made me lose respect for my old man. What was there to look up to, I thought, when he lets her treat him that way?

I guess my mom thought that by rubbing his nose in it, she'd get my dad to face up to his failures. But it never worked. He had talent, creative ability, and that famous artistic temperament. But he couldn't, or wouldn't, make it pay. Sometimes I get the feeling that if she had just let go and put all the responsibility in his hands, instead of taking it on herself, that he would have grown out of his fantasy world and into the real one. But, just like him, she couldn't change who she was: a fixer. She never saw the fear and insecurity behind her need, but the rest of us did. It was like living with a sick person, sick in a compulsive way, a way that gets things done, but still sick.

Frances and Pasquale didn't so much solve their problems as live with them. Or try to. There wasn't much heart-to-heart in my house. We just didn't know how to handle our emotions. If anyone tried to speak up about how they felt, about what was wrong, they were told that they shouldn't feel that way. That it was wrong to feel that way. And after a while you started to doubt *what* you felt, your own hopes and your own fears, and you started trying to second guess everyone, what it was they really wanted from you. You learned not to talk about what you were feeling and after a while you learned to stop feeling altogether. There was always someone in my life I was being measured against, some neighborhood success story I was supposed to model myself after. Who I really was wasn't ever good enough; the way I combed my hair, the way I walked and talked, and, later, the way I sang and stood on stage. There was always something to be improved, something to be fixed. Later, I heard about the term "low self-esteem." Back then, I just felt bad about being Dion. And mad at the people in my life who made me feel that way.

My grandfather, and all my uncles, disapproved strongly of my mother marrying a layabout like Pasquale DiMucci, but there was something about that charming, eccentric, interesting guy that made her fall in love. Some part of that love pulled them through, I think, even though you can't get them to admit it. "We have our way," she says today. "We've learned how to accept. We're used to each other." It was more like a truce than a marriage, and sometimes I felt I was caught between the battle lines, in no-man's-land.

My mom taught me to be honest. My dad taught me how to steal. He'd take me to Alexander's and slip things into his pockets, giving me a wink like it was all a big game, a game I was supposed to enjoy as much as he did. Once, I remember, he got caught red-handed, walking out of the store wearing a jacket with the price tags ripped off. The store detective nailed him and my dad spun the most amazing tale right on the spot, making up a story about his sick wife and his starving little son, and there I was trying to look pathetic and hungry. They actually let him go. It was one more thing that was supposed to make me proud. But it only confused and scared me. I wanted someone to look up to, not play games with.

My dad never disciplined me. He'd beat me, but it was only out of his own anger, and when you're a kid, you know the difference. It was the same with my sisters. Joanie and Donna. It got to where I was the father figure in their life and even though I did the best I could, I could never fill those shoes. But someone had to do it, and Pasquale, well, he just never learned how to really communicate with his kids, to motivate us. So we pretty much did our own thing, the best we could, and hoped that it would all work out. Sometimes I'd try to make a game out of all the chores that needed to be done to keep our home going. With my mom working all day, it was up to us to get the place neat and clean with food on the table and I used to pull all kinds of stunts, like a Bronx Tom Sawyer, to get my sisters to pitch in.

It was a lot of pressure, a lot of responsibility, and underneath it all was the fear that it all would explode. I wanted order and peace so bad because there wasn't any in my life. I got into shouldering responsibility to cover for my dad; if I could make the house spotless and my sisters behave, then my mom wouldn't have reason to remember how much her life had disappointed her. I did it out of love, I thought, but behind that love was guilt and resentment.

There was constant friction in the house between my mom and dad—arguing and recriminations and bitter tears. She was trying to teach responsibility and control and his attitude was, hey, we can always go on welfare. Sometimes it could bring down your whole world, like when my dad went to Europe with his puppets to try to make a name for himself. He was gone a year, and even though I remember it as one of the most peaceful times in my life, I still missed him. He was supposed to send money home from his shows, but, of course, it didn't work out that way and, in the end, my mom had to pay for his return ticket. We met him at the dock and I'll never forget the excitement I felt at seeing him again, at having the family back together. He came down the gangplank all smiles and jokes, wearing a hand puppet and pulling everyone's leg. We got into the cab and my mom started on him, screaming and yelling the whole way home about how he was a no-good bum, how he'd deserted his family, and, finally, inevitably, how he would never amount to anything. Something in me snapped at that moment. I think I realized, down deep inside, that it was never going to be the way I wanted. No matter how hard I tried, I could never fix them.

The arguing continued for days, and it got to where I'd climb out of bed and try to be louder than they were, as if that might snap them out of it. I didn't, but I finally found something that did, at least for a moment. My dad had brought a beautiful set of handpainted china dishes home with him from England. It was kind of his way of telling Frances that he really did care, and even in the midst of all that fighting, she cherished that set, putting them in a white cabinet in the kitchen for everyone to see. Well, one morning I got up and they were at it again, yelling and pointing their fingers and blaming each other and the world. I calmly walked over to that cabinet, my mom's pride and my dad's token of love, and pushed it over. It fell to the floor with a deafening crash, shattering the dishes, and with them, any dreams I had of living in a happy home, with happy parents, happily ever after.

CHAPTER 3

Luke the Drifter

I CAN still smell the aroma of my mother's spaghetti sauce, simmering on the stove for that Sunday supper. It was a beautiful, clear day, the sky blue and bright outside my bedroom window. I was ten years old, dreaming ten-year-old daydreams with my chin on the windowsill and the sun on my face. The year was 1949 and the war, a war I was barely old enough to remember, was over. Something was in the air—a change or the promise of a change—and if you sat real still and listened hard you could just catch it, that whisper that comes from something brand new and completely unexpected.

I heard it coming over the radio, drifting down the hall like the scent of my mom's good sauce. Outside, the neighborhood dozed through the Sabbath, but inside, my heart was pumping with excitement. I got up, pulled along by that sound, strange and distant and cut through with static. I went into the kitchen, and put my ear against the radio's small speaker. The look on my face must have been one of curiosity and pure pleasure and that kind of wonder only a kid can feel. Mom kept cooking, I guess, and Donna or Joanie may have come in to help. To tell you the truth, if there'd been a five-alarm fire with engines racing down Crotona Avenue, I don't think I would have noticed. I was listening, for the first time in my life, to the music of Hank Williams.

The voice was piercing and strong, forceful and very committed. He would attack a lyric and bite the end of his words off with a country twang that sounded like a foreign language and every once in a while it would break into a few thrilling falsetto notes. The pedal steel made a high, lonesome sound while the guitar strummed a deliberate, steady rhythm. I didn't know a thing about "that lonesome whippoorwill" or "the midnight train, whinin' low" but the first time I heard "I'm So Lonesome I Could Cry" I knew exactly what that tall drink of Alabama water was singing about.

I guess it happens mostly when you're young, when you're too dumb to know there's some things you're not supposed to like. I guess you have to be ten years old, wide open and willing to pick up on a sound that might as well have been from the moon, for all it had to do with the heart of the Italian Bronx. I guess what I'm saying is that I really didn't care. It didn't matter who was making that music, or how far away from my world he was. When I heard Hank Williams moan the country blues, it was like he was singing just for me.

On the face of it, I admit, there was no way I was supposed to pick up on the appeal of country music's greatest pioneer. After all, he was born in a two-room sharecropper's shack below the Mason-Dixon Line. He first started singing in railroad camps and drank his share of moonshine in roadhouses across the South. His audience was the dirt farmers, the hillbillies, the redneck crackers who'd never seen a two-story building, much less the towering skyscrapers of Manhattan. He was American, just like me, but that only went to show how big the country was and how many neighborhoods, how many pockets and corners it really had.

On the other hand, here was a guy whose mom had bought him his first guitar before he was ten. His father, a shell-shocked veteran of the war, had committed himself to a hospital and left his wife to support a son and daughter. And there was one other thing I had in common with the stranger: a love for music and singing. Hank Williams knew what it was like to have folks in the palm of his hand simply by the sound of his voice. It was something I was learning, too.

Hank Williams was twenty-six years old when I first heard him on the Don Larkin's show out of New Jersey. He had three years left of a short, sad, and shining life. I don't know whether or not he realized just how far his music reached, or the kind of people who made it their own. All I know is, on that Sunday morning, my world suddenly had a new horizon.

Like I said, my love affair with music, all kinds of music, had started early. Because my dad considered himself in show business, he went out of his way to cultivate show business friends and acquaintances, bringing them over for dinner, introducing them to the wife and kids. Among the jugglers, magicians, comics, and fellow puppeteers, there was a guy named Vinnie who came home with him one night and sang some barroom songs with the guitar at the kitchen table. I couldn't believe the way the whole room filled with music, making the hairs on the back of my neck stand on end. It happened every time I'd hear someone who knew what he was doing, who could warble the melody just right, wringing out the drama or the joy of an old Italian standard or some hit-parade favorite. Even on the street, when some drunk let loose with a dirty saloon song, I'd be listening, not just for the musical punchline, but to hear how well the guy could fit his voice to the melody.

Music came to me from all over the place. If I wasn't making it myself, on the stoop with Ricky, my cousin Pee Wee, Ronnie Greco, and the others, I'd be standing backstage at one of my dad's shows up in the Catskills, listening to some jug-eared crooner trying to give Sinatra a run. All my aunts had real musical talent, especially the youngest, Josephine. She'd take the stage at a talent contest or church dance and you could just tell she had it. She even went out on the road with my dad—brought along her own lights and wore these spangled dresses, doing Lena Horne or Judy Garland, Peggy Lee or Evelyn Knight. But she decided she didn't like the grind or the low lifes that were part of the business. All she really wanted was to love a man and raise a family.

I even picked up some blues from an old black guy named Willie, who used to do janitor work in the neighborhood bars. I'd hang out with him while he was sweeping and mopping and I'd soak up all the heartache of those great blues riffs, swaying and stomping to Willie's renditions of Big Bill Broonzy, Jimmy Reed, or John Lee Hooker.

But Hank Williams, well, Hank was different. From that Sunday on, I had to hear more. The very next day, I put together all my nickels and dimes and headed down to the local record store on Fordham Road. I plunked my money down and walked away with a fistful of Hank's singles—classics like his first big hit "Move It On Over," "Lovesick Blues," "Mind Your Own Business," and, of course, "I'm So Lonesome I Could Cry." I didn't just listen to them, I swallowed them whole, studying every bent note, the subtle interplay of the instruments, the plaintive catch in his throat. And, because I owned my own, I studied the way Hank brought his guitar up out of the background to fill in the harmonies along with his voice.

It was like I'd found a secret, a treasure from a faraway land that belonged just to me. I became a regular at the record shop after that and it got to where the owners, Mr. and Mrs. Donatello, would know to call me up whenever something new from that hillbilly singer was delivered. Of course, once I discovered Hank Williams, I started exploring other country recording stars, guys like Lefty Frizzell and Carl Smith, who had a five-minute show every day after school. I'd run home as fast as I could to catch him do two quick numbers, but to tell you the truth, the only reason I listened to others was because Hank wasn't making enough music to suit me.

There was something about the sound of his songs, a homemade quality that reminded me a little of the off-the-cuff stuff I was doing on the front stoop. Hank seemed to be saying that, if you had the talent, it wasn't all that hard. You could strum a chord and make it go on for days and with two chords, well, you could write your own song. To say he inspired my own music making doesn't go far enough; without Hank Williams, I'm not so sure I ever would have realized that music was my gift, too—my way of reaching people.

Of course, I sent off to his fan club and used to write

to the Grand Ole Opry to find out when he'd be on the air again. By the time I was thirteen I had nearly everything he'd ever recorded. And I could sing it. By heart. I started by picking out the few chords I recognized on my guitar and the rest just came naturally. I could serve up a respectable rendition of "Hey, Good Lookin'," "Honky Tonk Blues," or "Your Cheatin' Heart" and the funny thing was, the kids in the neighborhood couldn't get enough. It didn't matter that they'd never heard of Hank Williams, or that it was maybe the first time they'd ever heard a country twang, even if it was cut with a Bronx accent. They just loved to hear me do those "funny songs," almost as much as I loved to do them.

With music I felt part of something. I felt connected. I guess by the time I was a teenager I was beginning to realize the limits that were put on me by my family, by the neighborhood. I began to lose that sense of belonging that had carried me through my childhood and under-stand, deep down inside, that my parents' problems were taking their toll on me. Without even realizing it, I was looking for a way out.

Music seemed to offer that way. Singing a song, I felt special. And I knew people liked to hear what I did. Maybe music was going to be my ticket out. Maybe it could rescue me and along with me, my whole family.

Those kind of thoughts bring with them their own kind of pressure. Especially because my mom and dad started thinking the same thing. It started out as fun, with those Friday night concerts down at Ermondo's. I'd sing an old country drinking song and a couple of Hank's best and bring the house down. Pretty soon word got back to my folks, and, suddenly, I was being groomed. For what, I didn't know. And didn't want to know.

Anything that looked like an opportunity, my parents were there, dragging me along with my scrubbed face and slicked down hair. I guess the first time they tried to make something happen around me was when one of my dad's show biz contacts offered to book me at Fort Dix to entertain the GIs. I couldn't have been more than eleven years old and I was scared to death, standing on the stage of the enlisted men's club with all these drunk soldiers shouting and laughing at me. Somehow I managed to squeak out a version of "Kaw-Liga" and it was like the roof had fallen in. They went crazy and wouldn't let me go until I sang every song I knew, including some of those dirty Italian ones. Finally, they pulled me off the stage and carried me around on their shoulders, like some conquering hero, which was exactly how I felt.

After that, well, I guess my folks started seeing me as a ticket to the big time. They dressed me up in a straw hat and gingham cowboy suit, sat me down on a bale of hay with my guitar around my neck, and took a bunch of publicity shots, trying to pass me off as a country boy wonder. For a while, it looked like it was going to work. My dad took me down to a couple of radio shows, including Paul Whiteman's program, to show off his new discovery. I even made an appearance on *The Star Time Kids* where I met Connie Francis. I'd sing my Hank songs and strum my guitar and smile my dimpled smile and everyone seemed to think I had what they called "a future."

To say I was underwhelmed is putting it mildly. Sure, I enjoyed the attention, but at the same time there was a bell going off in the back of my brain, a feeling that people were using me for their own reasons. They were pushing me and it was in my nature to push back. Music was my thing. I didn't want anyone, least of all Pasquale and Frances, intruding. When I went off into a song, it was my own private world and I didn't need funny costumes or microphones or guest spots to make it real. It was mine, and as soon as I felt others trying to make it theirs, I backed off in a hurry.

It all came to a head when my dad took me down to the Roxy Theater to sing for Tony Bennett. I guess Bennett was the nearest thing to a real star that my dad had in his list of contacts and he was sure that Tony would flip over me. He wanted me to sing "Cold, Cold Heart," which had been a hit for Bennett, and made me get up on stage with my guitar and that stupid straw hat. He'd even brought down an agent from William Morris, but I didn't care. I just stood there stubbornly, staring at them all in stony silence with my dad threatening to kill me if I didn't open my mouth. But I wouldn't give him the satisfaction of turning my music into his meal ticket and after that I guess they didn't try so hard.

I was a headstrong kid, a little crazy, maybe, but I didn't care. I lived in my own world and it was comfortable there, comfortable and familiar. All of those big time opportunities didn't mean nearly as much to me as hanging out with Ricky and Pee Wee after *Your Show of Shows,* recreating all the skits, with Ricky doing Carl Reiner and me doing Sid Caesar and all the kids on the block as our audience. I was going to have it my way, or I wasn't going to have it at all. Sometimes I felt like the character Hank had created to sing his saddest songs, Luke the Drifter. In my mind he was kind of a ghost, invisible, floating above all the turmoil and trouble, making up music about what he saw and then drifting on, unattached, answering to no one.

Music set me up above it all, and by the time I was fifteen, music was crackling all around me. Getting turned on to Hank Williams had taught me early on that the best stuff wasn't always right under your nose, so I had an ear tuned to strange sounds that might give me the same charge. I was picking up influences from all over the place, mixing in early R&B with the doo-wop that seemed to be floating up from every street corner. Fats Domino, with his rolling, barrelhouse piano and cajun accent really gave me a jolt. So did Jerry Lee Lewis, Bo Diddley, and, of course, Elvis. In other words, like every other teenager in America, I was starting to discover rock 'n' roll.

CHAPTER 4

Susan

SHE came walking down the street, whispering and giggling with her friends, prim in her school clothes and trying to ignore the wolf whistles from the punks in front of Crazy Tony's. I caught sight of her as she rounded the corner, her arms full of books, and it was like something inside of me came alive. She was from another world, beyond the neighborhood, beautiful and full of promise.

Her name was Susan and she'd moved to the Bronx in 1954 from Vermont. I had no idea they grew anything as gorgeous as Susan up there. She was her father's only daughter, fresh and favored, and she had a clean, country air that followed her down the street like a summer breeze. She had freckles and flaming auburn hair, clean features and a flat, funny way of talking. One thing for sure; she wasn't Italian. Susan stuck out from the other girls like a torch in the dark and all I knew was that I had to get next to her. I was fifteen the first time I laid eyes on Susan. I fell head over heels in love.

I guess you could say things weren't so simple for me anymore. When I first met Susan I wasn't a kid, but I sure wasn't grown up. School was a waste of time, less of an education than a jail term. I'd already been pegged as a dreamer. Now I was getting a reputation as a trouble-maker and my mother finally decided she had to do something. I was shipped out to my Uncle Frank's in Bergenfield, New Jersey. He was supposed to be a stern disciplinarian—just the guy to whip me into shape.

I liked Bergenfield and hanging out with my two cousins; it was like having brothers. But somehow I still wasn't making the right impression. Even though my school work improved, the people in town didn't like the idea of having a "troubled" kid from New York corrupt-ing their youth. I danced a little too close with the local girls and my hair was combed a little too sleek and shiny. They got together a committee and told Uncle Frank, none too politely, to send me back where I belonged.

There was no doubt where that was—the streets. More and more it was the place I called home, and it wasn't long after I'd gotten back that Ricky and I decided to join the Fordham Daggers, the gang that claimed our neighborhood as its turf. It's another one of those clichés that I actually lived through. You know the image, from *West Side Story, Rebel Without a Cause,* and a dozen B-picture melodramas—the black leather jacket, Luckies in the T-shirt sleeve, and a tattoo that read "Live Fast, Die Young, and Leave a Good-Looking Corpse." I'm not sure if Hollywood was copying us or the other way around, but I do know that behind that myth was a reality, a reality that caught us up and sometimes carried us away.

We went to the Daggers' leader, a guy named Bruno, and told him we wanted in. Fine, he said, all we had to do was pass the initiation: three punches in the stomach from each member and an hour in the sewer,

hanging from the manhole ladder. I didn't think I was
going to make it, especially after one of the guys aimed
his punch a little low, but I took it like a man and became
a Dagger.

At least I tried. I wanted to be tough, and I wanted
to be part of something, and I had that kind of crazy
energy that makes you do dangerous and stupid things.
But I always felt like I was playing a part. Most of these
guys—Sammy Savage, Louie Spike, Tony, Tozzo,
Moach, Cheeks—were mean and hard and it came natural for them. Later, Tony even went to the top of Golden
Gloves. But for me, being in a gang was just one more
thing I was expected to do. I didn't have enough of an
idea about who I was to decide whether I really wanted
to be a part of that scene. It was what was required and I
followed along, hoping, maybe, no one would notice I was
faking it.

But it was no play acting. The trouble we caused ourselves and others was real. We didn't steal hubcaps or
terrorize old ladies. It wasn't like that. We'd come together to protect the turf, a few blocks of tenements we
called our own and staked out against the other gangs:
the Imperial Hoods or the Italian Berrettas or the Golden
Guineas. It was like kids drawing double-dare lines in the
schoolyard, and what seemed so important then just
seems sort of pathetic now. The fights we got into would
be about dumb things like insulting someone's girlfriend
—desperate attempts to stir things up, get something
going, just to feel something. I belonged all right, but
even then I kept asking myself, "Who am I?" "Why am I
here?" "Where am I going?"

Where a lot of guys went was to the grave. Our rum-
bles were mostly just punch-outs, but some guys, the

ones who played for keeps, carried knives. And, sometimes, guns. By the time Ricky and I left the Daggers to join the Baldies, a bigger, tougher local gang that took its name from the American eagle, we'd been to more than our share of funerals. Zip gun fights, car crashes, knife wounds, a drunken stunt that went way wrong: Friends of mine were checking out and nobody was asking why.

Then, suddenly, there was Susan. I approached her like I approached everything else in my life, with a mixture of sheer bravado and quaking fear. I wanted her to love me back, even just a little, but more than that I wanted her to look up to me. And admiration was something I thought I knew how to get. So I sang. I used to play school dances at the parish hall, Saint Martin of Tours, where Susan would come to hang out. I'd get up there and do my best Little Richard or Fats and look her right in the eyes. After a while she started looking back. Later, in the backseat of a car, we listened to the Flamingos, the Moonglows, the Five Satins, songs that became the backdrop for our romance, along with millions of other teenage dreamers.

But it wasn't a dream. Susan and I began a courtship that lasted eight years and took us through those intoxicating first days of major musical success. A lot happened in that time—in my career and between the two of us—and by some miracle we survived it all. Actually, it was less a miracle than, like I said, Susan's high tolerance for unacceptable behavior. My behavior. She was my high school sweetheart, sure, and we did a lot of growing up together, but that never would have pulled us through the tough spots. It was Susan's patience, her faith in some future that I couldn't even see, that was like the calm center of a very scary storm.

Her life hadn't exactly been a bed of roses up to that point, either. Jack, her father, was a heavy drinker. He'd moved the family to New York to take a job as a headwaiter in a Manhattan restaurant. Divorced and remarried, Susan's dad had trouble making ends meet. Moving from the country to the city, especially a tough neighborhood like ours, struggling with the bills—it was a big adjustment. But even then, at fifteen years old, she had a special kind of strength. It was like she shared the same joy for life, an ability to accept things as they were, that I'd had when I was a kid. Only, when I forget what it was like, she still remembered. That gave her strength. It was a strength I'd come to depend on. And, sometimes, take for granted.

Susan returned my love, just like in those great old songs. We went steady and then, after a while, it was more than steady. Both of us knew that this was for keeps. We didn't question it. I'm not saying that there weren't times when either one of us wanted out. But what we found in each other, even though we didn't know what to call it, was commitment. A reason to believe.

These were the melodies, light and dark, that were playing through me as I reached out to grow up. The gang, my girlfriend, my music: I wasn't so different from any other kid who thought tomorrow would never come.

Except, maybe, in one way. I was afraid of tomorrow, driven by fears that I couldn't name. Only feel. Love, for me, was respect and there was nothing I wanted more. My father's life haunted me, a gnawing feeling in the pit of my stomach whenever I thought I might lose face the way he had. For him, it just rolled like water off a duck's back. But I was different. No one would take advantage of me: No one would ever call me a fool. I wanted to have it all together, the way that no one ever has it all together, with every angle figured, every risk worked out, and everybody in line. Some people can make that work for them. For me, the fear that it wouldn't was overwhelming. For me, escape was the only answer.

I learned to find my way around reality at an early age. Drinking, naturally, was a part of the culture I was born into: Tony's wine and 7-Up spritzers is only one example. Then there was the time me, Pee Wee, Ricky, Ronnie Greco, and Tony Malazo all decided to get sauced for the first time. Aside from giving voice lessons, Ricky's dad also owned a liquor store, and we all used to go down to the basement to lift weights. One weekend his dad went away and we got into the gin stock. We took two quarts and started gulping, but it tasted so bad no one could get it down. So we bought some chocolate syrup, mixed one part gin to three parts Bosco, held our nose and chug-a-lugged. We ended up in the laundromat, stuffing clothes, and each other, in the dryers and thinking it was the funniest thing since Groucho Marx. A cop finally came in and Pee Wee—the shortest kid on the block—grabbed his hat and led him on a wild goose chase through the neighborhood. We laughed so hard our guts hurt, but that was nothing compared to how we felt the next morning.

I was about twelve that first time I got drunk, and a year later I smoked grass for the first time. Like drinking, it was part of the scene, something you were expected to do. I smoked and drank because it showed I was a man and, at the same time, I felt my fear shrink when I was high. The world seemed like a brighter place, less grim and threatening. Most important, I didn't care so much if things weren't how I thought they should be. I felt good and that was a change from how I felt most of the time, when I was alone with myself.

You can't have that kind of experience without it changing something inside you. You get drunk and pull a few pranks and the next time the old lady's screaming at the old man, the next time some guy calls your bluff on the street, the next time you start to wonder if your girlfriend really loves you, well, you remember what feeling good was like.

But reefer and booze was nothing compared to what smack did for me. I first snorted heroin when I was fourteen going on fifteen. I don't remember where I got the stuff, probably because at that time, it had become so common on the streets and in the gangs. In one way you could say that junk broke up the gangs. When you were really high, the last thing you wanted to do was look for trouble. It was a chemical straight jacket, cooling you out, creating its own sense of serenity and peace, and a lot of other things I was missing in my life.

Heroin was instant courage. It was freedom like I'd never had. It was complete confidence: a magic potion that set the world right side up. Smack did for me what I couldn't do for myself. I wasn't afraid any longer. My doubts disappeared in a warm, embracing glow. That first time I did it, I remember walking down Crotona Avenue in the middle of the street, on the white line, and looking up at the tenement buildings. I felt like it all belonged to me, like I owned the world and it was a beautiful place.

I didn't need to be afraid of people anymore. I could move right up to the girl I loved, in front of everyone outside the candy store, and I could spin a spell with my words. It was impossible to say the wrong thing. I was the hippest, handsomest, most together cat on the block, the best dancer, the sharpest dresser; I knew it and it was only a matter of time before she would, too.

That's how it felt, anyway, like living in a world that suddenly made sense. The day I took heroin was the day I began dreaming really big, about my career, about Susan, about getting out and making something of myself. I had the power. I was fortified. The world was mine, just waiting to be cracked open and enjoyed, like a ripe melon.

You figure it out. I'll never know why some powder could make so much difference in the way I felt and looked at things. But it did and once you had a taste of that reality, you never forgot it. It was like my life suddenly split in two, dividing into the times I was high and the times I wasn't. The high times swallowed up whatever was left of those simple pleasures that had once been mine and replaced them with a single sensation, the pure rush of the drug, coursing through my veins. There's nothing like it and I guess there never will be, which is probably why junkies spent their lives dedicated to that rush, better than a woman, better than money, better than love.

It didn't take me long to discover that junk also enhanced my stage performance, too. I'd kind of slide into a song, hunch my shoulders over, close my eyes and feel the music well up from deep in the pit of my stomach. There was a weight and warmth to the notes that I'd never heard before, a thousand special moments tied up in a single refrain. Nothing had ever felt so absolutely right. This is what I'd been born for, what I'd been waiting so long for.

Of course, no matter how good I felt, I wasn't anxious for anyone else to find out what I was up to. There was a real stigma attached to any kind of hard drug use, and I remember my mom warning me away when I was little. It was dangerous, she said, addictive. You could get hooked, and once a junkie, always a junkie. I saw *The Man with the Golden Arm* and heard all the horror stories. But for me, junk was the key and I wasn't going to let go. I understood immediately how someone could get strung out, just wanting to be in that beautiful world all the time, so I consciously regulated myself. I had a calendar in my room and I charted the days I got stoned, which were usually on the weekend. At first I was able to keep it down to a couple of times a week, but after a while any thought of control was a joke.

Don't get me wrong. I wasn't crawling through alleys, robbing liquor stores for a fix. I had it more together than that. At least I thought I did. But that's the biggest lie of all, the soft voice that leads you, one step at a time, into the nightmare. Junk was like my secret lover—an affair that I kept from everyone close to me, including Susan.

It was a little harder to keep it from Ricky. After all, we ran in the same gang, down streets that had no secrets. Ricky never got into drugs and when he found out what I was doing he got mad. Really mad. He caught me down on the corner one evening, grabbed me by the shirt collar, and slammed me against a brick wall. Eye to eye he told me I didn't know what I was doing, and it wasn't gentle persuasion. He was burning up, threatening to flatten my nose. It was out of love that he put our friendship on the line. He wanted to scare some sense in me, but you can't scare a junkie. I just smiled and shook him off and told him to be cool. As cool as I was.

I knew junk was wrong, in the same way I knew stealing and cheating was wrong. From a distance. But I didn't lose any sleep over it, because, suddenly, there were people around me, important people, telling me I was doing everything just right.

CHAPTER 5

The Belmonts

CARLO Mastrangelo. Fred Milano. Angelo D'Aleo. They were the best in the neighborhood, maybe the best in the Bronx, and back then, in the middle of the Fifties, there was lots of competition for that crown. Seems like every street corner had its own harmonizing heroes back then; guys who would spend hours getting down their parts, riffing off the big doo-wop hits of the day and dreaming, just maybe, that if they got good enough, if they could whip up that slick a cappella blend like topping on a sundae, it might just be their voices coming off the radio from a fire escape on a hot summer night.

Carlo, Freddie, and Angelo. I'd sung with them dozens of times on the front stoop or stopped on my way somewhere to take the lead on "Earth Angel," "I Love You So," or "Story Untold" underneath the streetlight. They were guys who'd drifted in and out of my scene for years, not close friends, not like Ricky, but guys you'd shout hello to from down the street. And who'd shout back.

The name they took was the Belmonts, after Belmont Avenue, and the music we made together was the pure sound of the neighborhood. It wasn't born in the studio, or in some songwriter's cubbyhole downtown in the Brill Building. We didn't cook up a style or try to second guess the record-buying public. We sang what made us happy, and it just turned out that it made a lot of other people happy, too. The way we worked was the way we'd always worked, by instinct. And our instincts were good. Sure. I was up front. I had a lot of ideas, and I was the one really looking for it all to happen. But Carlo, Freddie, and Angelo were the other three quarters of a real musical partnership. We were a team, and it got so where we could anticipate each other's best riffs. Our music was born out of just being compatible; one guy would start humming a melody, another would join in, and a song would take shape, something bigger and more satisfying than just the sound of four voices on the street— something we could be proud of.

Freddie and Carlo had been in the Imperial Hoods for a while, knocking around the neighborhood with that same mix of boredom and excitement that sparked us all. Along with Angelo and me, there was a real pool of talent in that foursome, a lucky blend of natural ability. Angelo had actually had some operatic training when he was younger, as well as the gift of perfect pitch. Not that it seemed so wonderful when we were all working out our harmonies and he was the only one on the note. But we learned to key to him, like a human tuning fork. Carlo, when he wasn't singing, had worked up some mean chops as a jazz drummer and was the first guy I ever knew who

really wrote a song. That impressed me. I mean, I knew
a guy who could put the words and the melody together
and make it sound good. One of his earliest numbers, I
remember, was called "We Went Away." Freddie? Well,
Freddie was a rock 'n' roll freak with a flair for getting
down the fundamentals. The music we sang was basically
doo-wop with all the seamless harmonies and vows of
eternal love that made that music an American classic.
We mixed in some R&B, early rock 'n' roll, blues, songs
we were hearing on the radio and from other groups on
the street. When we got together, we felt good about ourselves, showing off like kids playing "look, ma, no
hands!" And people dug our stuff.

When I first pulled them together and the Belmonts
and I started singing seriously, as a group, we'd rent
some cold water flat by the week and just hole up, working on numbers and polishing the act. But anywhere
would do, when you got right down to it: hallways, play-
grounds, alleyways. A lot of our rehearsing was on the
Sixth Avenue D train, heading downtown. We'd grab a
couple of seats and start banging out time on the floor.
Trains had the greatest bass sound in the world. So did
the back seats of Checker cabs, underneath the El, or on
the roof of a building, next to the pigeon coops.

People in the neighborhood couldn't wait to hear the
latest thing we'd cooked up. They bragged about us, encouraged us, and respected us, which for me was the
most important thing of all. Our success was their success,
but it was funny. When we started making records they
were also some of our biggest critics. They always felt
we'd loused up the songs, that they were better fresh off
the street. They'd take our new 45 and play it on some
rinky-dink machine and hit their heads with the palms

of their hands, shouting about how we'd ruined our sound. One thing we learned real quick: You can't please everyone.

Even without my mom and dad pushing, I guess it was inevitable that I'd take a shot at recording sooner or later. When it came, it seemed almost accidental. There was a guy in the neighborhood named Johnny, who few of us took for real. We all goofed on him, but he had a brother, Phil, a songwriter, who he always bragged about. No one even believed him, I think, except my dad, who was always on the lookout for an opening. He talked me in to going down and meeting Johnny's brother, who turned out not only to be for real, but who also had some real good tips.

It was Phil Noto who introduced me to Bob and Gene Schwartz, hardworking accountants and wide-eyed newcomers in the rough-and-tumble world of the record business. Things were different in those days, and you could put out real records without a whole lot of money. Of course, it took a whole lot *more* money to get those records played on the radio, but Bob and Gene figured they'd cross that bridge when they got to it. They'd had the itch for quick bread and a little fun, like some of the music clients in their accounting business. They set up shop as Mohawk Records on West Fifty-fourth Street and waited for the hits to roll in. They were what we called square back then, with crew cuts and bow ties and big, thick glasses.

But they knew music. I auditioned for Gene Schwartz, more for my dad's sake than anything else, doing my version of "Wonderful Girl," the old Five Satins' chestnut. It was my favorite song at the time, kind of a dedication to Susan. I played and sang and, for some reason, gave it my best shot. I guess I just figured it was no use fighting my dad anymore, cutting off my nose to spite my face. Sure, he was working the angles, but who's to say those angles couldn't work my way, too?

Gene didn't say "Come here, boy, I'm gonna make you a star," but it amounted to the same thing. The Schwartz brothers would give me a try. I think I was the second singer they'd signed. It was 1957 and I was eighteen years old. What did I have to lose?

Gene sent me home with a backing track that day, a tape with all the instruments and background vocals, but no lead. I was supposed to learn the song and come back in a couple of weeks to record it. Only one problem: The tracks were sterile and sweet and—there's only one word for it—square, with this group called the Timberlanes crooning in the background like a barbershop quartet. I told them what I thought and they said "cut it anyway," and something told me I should do it.

It was called "The Chosen Few," Mohawk Records number 105. Don't ask me what the other 104 were. I guess no one was more surprised than I was when it showed up on the radio. I was happy just to have a piece of plastic with a hole in the middle and my name on it: Dion and the Timberlanes. I was naturally the talk of the neighborhood, and I milked it for everything it was worth, even though I was still kind of embarrassed by those old fogies, the mysterious Timberlanes, backing me on the song. I never did meet those guys and it was only later that I found out the conductor on the backing track sessions had been Hugo Montenegro. He also put together the orchestration for the flip side, a real slice of hokum called "Out in Colorado," which sounded like something you'd hear piped on a Wild West ride at Palisades Park. No hard feeling, Hugo. It was just that I knew guys on the block, lots of guys, who could sing rings around the Timberlanes.

Rings or not, "The Chosen Few" actually cracked a few markets. Boston, to be exact, which I never could understand. I'd never been to Boston. Who was listening up there and why? I was actually a star somewhere and while I may not have been the next Elvis, you couldn't tell it by me. I had a hit, man, at least in Boston, and as soon as I saw that opening, that opportunity, I went for it. I quit school so I could spend all my time developing a "career."

It really wasn't much of a choice. School for me was a lost cause, anyway. I'd come in the morning, go to a few classes, get into a fight in the lunch room, and walk out of the place like a big shot. I knew more than they could ever teach me, anyway. I'd already been bounced from seven different high schools and none of them were any different. I was a dreamer, restless and, most important, going places. The teachers were jerks if they couldn't see my potential. I'd hang around on the street until the bell rang, walk Susan home, and then try to round up some money for a nickel bag. The gang, the street corner singing, the big dreams with me and my girl. What did I have to hold me back? Mohawk Records and "The Chosen Few" might not have been the brass ring, but it was all I had and I was going for it.

I don't know if I ever really looked past what was happening right in front of me. Did I want to make a career of singing? Did I think I was good enough? Did I know anything about the business? None of that really mattered. I was flying high by the seat of my pants, and it felt good. Like I really was going places. The rest would just take care of itself.

As much as possible, I wanted to pick my shots. I knew I'd have to dump the Timberlanes, whoever they were, and replace them with guys who had their chops down, who could really deliver. You want to hear some stuff, I asked Gene? I'll show you some stuff. He laughed and agreed to give it a try, and the next day I was back with Angelo, Carlo, and Freddie. We ran some of our street corner shuffle past Gene and, bow tie, horn rims, and all, he went for it. He'd take a shot with the Belmonts.

For the guys, it was all kind of new, but I was beginning to pick up on the possibilities. We started rehearsing new material, and I was the one who drove round to pick them up in my old Kaiser. It really took determination, especially since each guy lived on the top floor of his building. I'd shake them out of bed, pour some coffee down their throats, and get them to the rehearsal hall. This is really important, I kept telling them. I was the driving force and it was the biggest challenge in my life. I wanted so badly to take control, to force it to happen, but I knew it wasn't going to fall into my lap. I thought I had what it took, my voice and the driving need to succeed. And maybe that was gonna be enough.

I think Carlo, Angelo, and Freddie took it all a little easier. It was a lark and it sure beat working in a shoe store or gas station, but the best thing about it was the way it impressed the girls. Man, I can remember those early sessions. We'd jump on the train, me with Susan and the rest with their steadies, and head down for the studio, bursting in like a party on wheels with bags of hero sandwiches and sodas. Gene would blow a fuse, try-ing to get us to work. "What are you eating?" he'd shout. "You'll ruin your voices!" And there we'd be, with spa-ghetti stains on our T-shirts, grinning at our girls. We were recording artists.

But, somehow, we got over. Being in a studio never really made me nervous. My approach to cutting records was, and still is, simple: Don't fake it. Standing in front of that microphone, I could shut my eyes and see the street corner where we'd first started singing. I could hear ev-eryone joining in, the girls clapping hands, and someone banging on a cardboard box. Sometimes it would be winter, bitter cold, but we'd still be out there, stamping our feet by an oil barrel fire. I could remember and hold on to just that feeling. The rest was easy: You open your mouth and let it come out.

It's a looseness, a way of enjoying the music that lets you sing the same song a hundred times and still do it different each time. I was glad people like Gene were around. I depended on them to get down on tape what was coming out of us. My job was to bring it out of my-self, like the impressionist painters I used to see at the museum when I'd be sitting on my dad's shoulders. See, he'd say, pointing to a picture by van Gogh. See, he doesn't even wait to put the paint on the brush. It goes straight from the tube to the canvas. He's expressing himself.

I knew just how van Gogh felt.

Mom and Dad walking on the boardwalk in Atlantic City, 1947

Mom and Dad in 1987 on their fiftieth wedding anniversary—still a good-looking couple

Me at age three with my first set of wheels

At twelve years old I got hooked on Hank Williams.

Singing Hank Williams's song "Cold, Cold Heart" to Tony Bennett during his appearance at Radio City Music Hall in 1954. Tony had made the song a big hit, but I knew I could sing it better.

Doing my Steve Reeves
pose in Bronx Park

At sixteen I was a member of a local Bronx
street gang called the Fordham Baldies.

Here I am looking cool on the corner of Crotona and 183rd Street.

My father took this picture of me in our kitchen using a sheet for the backdrop.

Bruno of Hollywood

The first tour picture of Dion and the Belmonts, 1958

With Dick Clark on "American Bandstand," 1959. It was the beginning of a long friendship.

Rick Guiliano and Judy with me and Susan at Bobby Darin's opening night at the Copa, 1960

With Sam Cooke; I loved making music with him.

Heading for Manhattan on the Third Avenue El

CHAPTER 6

I Wonder Why

WE got it in three takes, down at Allegro Studios, in the spring of 1958. It was one of those great sessions; we were picking up each other's cues like a quarterback with three great pass receivers and we gave the song all the street smarts we had. It was too long, I remember, and Gene had to cut it in the middle, but the only real trouble we had was with the tune's intro, which originally went something like "wella wella wella I don't know why . . ." and Carlo didn't want to do the "wellas." He didn't want to look like a jerk, he said, so we huddled and came up with a new intro. Gene, who was less interested in "wellas" than the price of the studios, said sure, do it, it's great. And we did.

We sang into one mike, each guy positioned according to how loud he was. Some of the studio cats that Gene hired for the session worked regularly for the Apollo stage band, career musicians who'd seen it all, from symphonies to Polish polka sessions. Like Buddy Lucas, the great one-eyed sax player who blew for the Belmonts and me on some big hits. He was big, too—250 to 300 pounds—and he loved to give us the benefit of his wisdom, whatever that might be. He taught my wife a great chicken recipe, for instance, a dish we call Chicken Buddy Lucas to this day. And for me there was plenty of sage advice. "Go down to the shore, Dion," he'd say. "If you think you're powerful, take a look at the ocean." Personally, I preferred the chicken, but what I liked best was the way Buddy played.

When we were done with "I Wonder Why," all of us—Gene, the Belmonts, the musicians, and I—knew there was something special about the tune and the way we'd cut it. The chiming spiral harmonies that opened it up, the fast-break vocal change-overs, the simple, driving rhythm—it all fell into place. And I can't say I wasn't thrilled to hear my own singing way out front, handling those rhythm breaks with the greatest of ease. This was the music I wanted to record, stuff I'd like to hear on the radio. I had another reason to be proud of the platter: The flip side, "Teen Angel," was my first shot at songwriting. It wasn't "Blue Suede Shoes," not even close, but it had verses and choruses and you could hum to it. What do you want for sixty-nine cents worth of plastic?

"I Wonder Why" was a real workout and a great showcase for what the Belmonts did best. It was also proof that Gene, who brought us the song from two Brill Building regulars, knew exactly what he was doing. It was two minutes and fourteen seconds of magic, and when I listen to it today, it's still something to be proud of. What it does for me, I think, is bring back just how exciting and innovative that time in music was. "I Wonder Why" wasn't anything more, or less, than the sounds we'd been doing on the street, rocking the cradle of that infant sound. In that way, it kind of reminds me of one of those African drum or Indian rain dance records: It's like some explorer went into a strange subculture in the middle of the city and came back with the latest from the natives. The song is fun and full of itself with an edge of nervousness and sheer adolescent energy. We'd hit it, right out of the box.

The tune was released on Laurie Records, which is the name Gene and Bob had chosen to replace Mohawk, and throughout the spring of that year "I Wonder Why" was all over the radio. At least it seemed that way to us. The song picked up stations in Boston, Philadelphia, Baltimore, New York—all up and down the eastern seaboard. It was a breaker and then, suddenly, it broke through on a ten-week run in the Billboard Top Twenty. But I'm sure if they'd been able to chart it by neighborhood, Crotona Avenue and 187th would have been the epicenter of the excitement. I'll never forget the first time we heard ourselves on the radio. We were so jazzed we bought spray paint and scrawled "Belmonts" on the back of our leather jackets, running down the streets and bouncing off the bumpers of cars, like something out of a Broadway rags-to-riches saga. We'd arrived, and as our ship pulled in it was like we were hauling a barge behind us, with the whole neighborhood on board, cheering. It was more than local boys making good. It was like we proved that our turf was the best. It was something we all shared: Joe the groceryman, the boys down at Tally's, Willie the janitor, Mike the stonecutter, all our girlfriends and brothers and sisters and everyone who'd known us since knee pants. "I Wonder Why" finally peaked in May of '58. By that time, Carlo, Freddie, Angelo, and I were living in a whole different world.

People say there's no such thing as an overnight success. Maybe, but Dion and the Belmonts got pretty close. I guess that's because, for us, fame, money, and a real future all came as such a complete surprise. It wasn't like we'd planned for years to break into the big time, as if this was the payoff for a life's work. We didn't even really try that hard. Rehearsing, for instance, was something we never did unless we absolutely had to. They wanted us to get some choreography going, and we'd check out all these great groups with their awesome moves, splits and twirls and kicks in time, like a chorus line. We knew there was no way we were going to match that, especially after they put us in a mirrored room and we got a chance to see what we looked like when we tried to dance together. So we decided to snap our fingers, which seemed much cooler anyway. That was our gimmick, the snapping group. When you get right down to it, we lucked out, which is to say, we had some talent, we made the most of it, and the breaks happened by themselves. It really *was* a million to one shot but, hey, someone had to be that one.

Don't misunderstand. What made the Belmonts get over was the simple fact that we were out front doing the kind of music teenagers loved to hear. It was fast and sharp, as cool as the clothes we started to wear: shiny nylon shirts, pegged pants with thin black belts, and low, Cuban-heeled shoes—what we called pimp boots. We took even more time combing our hair, if that was possible, and there was no mistaking the kind of looks we were starting to get on the street; from the boys, envy; from the girls, well, you figure it out.

And then there was the money. Royalties didn't start rolling in right away, but Gene was always willing to make an advance against future earnings and suddenly we had more than two pieces of silver to rub together. And with success came a squad of slightly shady guys, in shiny suits and wraparound shades and lots of papers to sign.

One of the first gigs we did after "I Wonder Why" was Dick Clark's "American Bandstand" right after it had gone from a local broadcast to the national airwaves. Clark brought us down to Philly, where the show was broadcast, and when we arrived backstage, with garment bags slung over our shoulder and nervous looks flickering between us, he went out of his way to make us feel at home. Dick, a little fresh faced and untried himself, was engaged in a battle to legitimize rock 'n' roll to the older generation. It was no easy job and I'm not so sure we were giving him any help.

By today's standards, of course, Dion and the Belmonts hardly made records parents wanted to burn. But there was something about the sight of those four Italians, decked out in city slicker clothes, snapping their fingers and acting like Negroes, that must not have set too well with the folks in the Midwest. We were kind of exotic, which, back then, meant foreign, and that, in turn, meant dangerous—a red light to the upstanding citizenry. As much as anything, that was part of our appeal. If only those mothers and fathers who shook their heads in disapproval *really* knew where we were from, and what we'd been up to. As it was, our strange, foreign-sounding music, our olive skin, and big city smirks were menacing enough.

Two things I remember about that first appearance on "Bandstand." First, the stage looked so much smaller than it did on TV, and, with the hot lights and the frantic pace, it was like an electric charge for us. Second, the crowd went wild. When Carlo launched into his new intro, "din, din, din, din," and we all snapped our fingers in time, the kids couldn't get enough. Clark may not have brought around the hardnoses, but he'd tapped into something hot. And that turned out to be a lot more important.

Fact was, "I Wonder Why" and Dion and the Belmonts surprised a lot of people. Another of our early, out-of-town gigs was at the Howard Theater in Washington, D.C., which was a totally black venue: artists, audience, ticket takers, the whole shot. They loved us. We had a two-week stand there, living in an all-black boarding-house, sleeping during the day, performing and partying with all our new friends during the night. We got the same response at the Apollo in Harlem where we were the first white performers ever to play the house. We'd hit the stage hard and confident, and in the minute it took for everyone to get over the shock that the guys who sang "I Wonder Why" weren't black, we were already off and running. Halfway through the show, I'd grab a guitar from the band and pluck out some honky-tonk riffs. We'd throw in old R and B, Little Richard, Chuck Berry, anything and everything and the crowd ate it up. We were even asked back for another week's run!

It was great fun. Everything was fun back then for four kids on a roll. It was all so new. I remember one day we bought some cool shoes in the heart of Harlem, white with jet black trim, real slick saddle shoes. That Friday night at the Apollo, the Belmonts and I hit the stage in a flash of energy, singing "I Wonder Why." Man, we were pumped up! As the band roared into the big ending, the audience jumped to its feet and we jumped into the move we'd worked out together for our finale, four quick steps back and a big bow. It was just about then that I noticed that Carlo had only one of his fancy white shoes on. On the other foot was a regular sneaker! The band started cranking up "No One Knows" but by that time it was too late. I was starting to laugh. I didn't know why he'd mixed his footwear like that, but just about then, it seemed like the funniest thing I'd ever seen. I started giggling, then howling, and the other guys, who'd also picked up on Carlo's peculiarity, caught the bug. Before we were four bars into the tune we were holding on to each other, trying to keep from falling over in hysterics. The band just kept playing through the laughter and somehow, the show went on.

Suddenly, nothing was the same anymore, but, at least in the beginning, nothing seemed that different either. I could look back just a few months before, when I'd been working part time for my Uncle John, the electrician. That life seemed like someone else's, but at the same time, if it wasn't me living out success, then who was it?

I was still Susan's steady, for instance, although I was content to leave it just that way. We'd double date with Ricky and his girl, Judy, the four of us taking a ride down to White Castle for a bag of burgers in my silver T-Bird with the black roof and the electric windows. My girl and I acted like the neighborhood king and queen. Which was pretty much what we were. I loved Susan, was still crazy about her, but I also thought I was a pretty great guy. I wanted my cake and, naturally, I wanted to eat it, too. So when other girls started showing a little interest, or a lot of interest, I'd try to oblige without Susan finding out. I stepped out on her, sure, and honestly couldn't see anything wrong with it. That was the code, the ethic of the street, and I wasn't about to buck tradition. Not when it was serving me so well.

The truth was, I was hiding from real love, real intimacy. I'd just back off whenever it threatened the way I liked things, which was always at arm's length. I never met Susan's family and never went out of my way to try. I didn't want to know any more about her than the part that was already familiar. No wonder it came as a complete surprise when she told me she was moving to Manhattan to take a job selling blouses in a department store. She rented an apartment and tried to settle into responsibility while she waited for me to make up my mind.

Susan was trying to hold on to what we had, even as I drifted further away into the fantasy of what my life was becoming. Like I said, she has a high tolerance, a tolerance that was only beginning to be tested.

At the same time, heroin was hanging on like a stubborn ghost, haunting my bright horizons. But even that had its romantic edge. The more musicians and singers I met, the more I realized how much smack was a part of the scene. We shared a gig with the great Frankie Lymon and the Teenagers, who'd hit the year previously with the smash "Why Do Fools Fall in Love." Small, wiry, and full of ambition, Frankie was a lot younger than I was and a lot deeper into drugs. He'd come down to the neighborhood at night sometimes and the two of us would get a couple of dime bags and do it up together. Later, lost in the shimmering haze of the high, we'd talk about music, trading licks, and building castles in the air. Frankie was another big dreamer, a guy who had his path to the top clearly laid out and that really impressed me. He was still a kid, but he knew just where he was going and just how to get there. Trouble was, heroin took him on a permanent detour. Years later, when I heard about Frankie's overdose, the end of another short, sad life, I felt a chill race up my backbone. It could've been me. It almost was me.

Suddenly our time didn't belong to us anymore, which suited the Belmonts and me just fine. Before "I Wonder Why" all we had was time: time to get into trouble, time to hang out, all the time in the world. Now we were always on the go, in the studio making records, on the radio doing interviews, on the road singing in front of people we'd never met before and would never see again. We did what we were told, what Bob and Gene and all the new guys in the sharkskin suits told us was best for our career. That kind of fame, coming at you all in a rush, can really throw you for a loop. One minute we were four mooks on the street, the next, everyone wanted to get close to us. It was like a narcotic, as strong, in its way, as anything I was putting in my veins. The lights, the crowds, the rush that hit you like a wave when we ran out from the wings and the applause came rushing over us—it was the same old story, told a million times before. But for us it was all happening for the very first time. You never wanted it to stop, and the only way to keep it going, it seemed to us, was to smile, sing, and try to sort it all out later. The music we were making was connecting and that was success, by any measure we knew. People—my family—were treating me like I was something special. I didn't have any trouble believing them.

When we weren't in the studio with Gene, cutting new material, we were onstage, playing a string of one-night stands up and down the eastern seaboard. The way we toured back then was in seven-week stints, three on, one off, three on. The Belmonts' first real road trip was a package deal with Bobby Darin, Jimmy Clanton, Joanne Cambell, and a couple of third and fourth-billed hopefuls.

Darin was only three years older than me, but he could have been my father, for all the know-how and experience he had. He'd just scored with "Splish Splash," but even then you could tell he had more on his wish list than just being a teen idol. When you travel hundreds of miles with a guy, eating bad food, sharing roach-infested hotel rooms, it goes without saying you get to know him. Bobby was one of the first real friends I had in the music business, someone who was on the same rung of the ladder as I was, but who took the time to give me the benefit of what he'd learned. He was a great person to be around—positive, fun, and extremely ambitious. He had to be. Bobby Darin knew he was living on borrowed time, convinced he wouldn't make it past thirty because of a bad heart, which had first been diagnosed when he was in the army. It was like a time bomb in his chest and it drove him to reach for the top before it went off.

It was Darin who taught me some fundamentals of the business side of music. Sitting on that bus while the miles between gigs rolled by, he took me under his wing, advising me to get a manager—someone who'd come up through the ranks and had drive. He also gave me tax tips, showing me how to keep a journal of expenses and figure royalty percentages. At the end of that first year I ended up paying Uncle Sam a couple of grand less than the Belmonts, using what Bobby had taught me.

He was also great fun to be around. I'll never forget the time the tour hit Akron and I was walking through town with some local girl after curfew. I think I was reciting poetry or something, but whatever it was, the cops didn't like it. They hauled me away to jail and the next morning Darin turns up with the entire tour behind him. The Belmonts were yelling at the cops, the cops were yelling back and Bobby's acting like Perry Mason, insisting on being my lawyer. For a minute there it looked like he might actually snow them, until the chief threatened to throw *him* in jail. I threw down bail and we were back on the road.

There were a lot of people like Darin coming into my life just then: interesting, educated, and exciting. Like Phil Spector. With his black cape and shades he could have been one of the neighborhood characters. He was in the Teddy Bears and his production work on their number one hit "To Know Him Is to Love Him" singled him out as the hottest new guy in town. I remember him coming down to the Apollo to check us out, little and squirrely, with a big nose and funny hair, the kind of guy that always got picked on where I came from.

Or like Sam Cooke, who we shared a bill with on a year-end tour. We did a swing through the South and the white guys in the bus had to get out at the stops to buy the black guys sandwiches and coffee from these little roadside dives. It was my first run-in with real racism and, being from New York, I thought it was outrageous. Cooke, too, was one in a million, a gentle, vulnerable guy, easy to be around and—with a voice honed and honeyed on the gospel circuit—easy to listen to. Man, I'd like to have tapes of what went on in some of those buses, with me and Sam and the Belmonts spinning our harmonies like silk along those empty roads. Sometimes Eddie Cochran would be on board. Sometimes Gene Vincent. Whoever it was, the music seemed like it would never end.

Yeah, it had all happened fast. But I was keeping right up, loving every minute of it. I was the new kid in a very elite club, rubbing shoulders with people who seemed very sophisticated and savvy. The fears in my life, the doubts and insecurities and pain, had been pushed back into some dark corner. It was like I was a kid again and everything was brand new and shiny. Now I knew how life was supposed to be. Just like in the movies.

CHAPTER 7

Winter Dance Party

1958 came and went like a burst of fireworks. The roller coaster ride wasn't stopping and, if anything, we'd never worked so hard in our lives. But it was the kind of gig that didn't seem like work. People were paid to say nice things about us—press agents, reporters, deejays—and we were getting paid for sounding and looking cool. Sure, we didn't own a minute or an inch of our lives. Sure, we were constantly blown out from traveling, tired, hoarse and a little hostile, but we'd also never had so much fun. So much expensive fun.

The stuff we were cutting with Gene was being released as follow-ups to "I Wonder Why." "No One Knows," a sleepy ballad with a torchlight treatment, cracked the Top Twenty. The flip side was one of the weirdest things we ever did, a version of Fats Domino's "I Can't Go On (Rosalie)" with Carlo actually singing Fats's piano part. Our third single, "Don't Pity Me," never made it past number forty. Maybe because, de-

spite the title, the tune dripped self-pity. I had a thing
about songs that made girls get sad.

Our first album was released in early 1959. *Presenting Dion and the Belmonts* produced our next two big
hits, starting with "A Teenager in Love," which Gene
had gotten from the writing team of Pomus and Shuman.
Mort Shuman is a real original, the first professional
songwriter that I ever hung out with and an amazingly
talented guy. He had a photographic memory, spoke
more than fifteen languages and sang in even more. He'd
take a guitar and suddenly become a flamenco virtuoso,
or sit down at the piano and transform himself into a Mississippi blues master. Later in his career he even trans-
lated the music of another real original, Jacques Brel,
and turned it into a Broadway hit. Mort had a huge circle
of friends, including Carole King, Otis Blackwell, Neil
Diamond; it was an education in entertainment. I started
collecting the demos these writers would produce to sell
their work and, for me, Mort Shuman's version of "You'll
Think of Me" even tops Elvis's.

Gene and I had put together the tune stack for that
first LP, and included all kinds of things. There was a
version of "Wonderful Girl," the song that got me signed,
a lightweight country tune called "You Better Not Do
That," and a real grab bag of other stuff.

With the release of that first album the money really
started coming in—more money than I'd ever seen in my
life. I bought my parents a big Buick and moved them
into a beautiful split-level house in White Plains. It was a
brand-new house in a brand-new development at the end
of a street with no name. For me, it felt like a new beginning. Like I was replaying my life the way it should have
been lived. With me as the hero. I was buying respect

and it was working. I told myself how much I liked helping people, how compassionate I was. I cared about people, which made me feel good about myself, about the
best son two parents ever had. I was fixing things up: Mr.
Fix-It.

I could have started with myself. Smack was the silent partner in everything I did, a way to regulate and
control a hectic scene. I depended on it to make things
sane. Or just to make things go away. Although Susan
and the Belmonts knew about my habit and I knew it
worried them, I hadn't changed much since the time
Ricky had shoved me against the wall. You still couldn't
tell me anything. I was using regularly, and not just heroin. Grass, pills, booze, they all had their purposes. My
calendar counter was long gone. I didn't want to remind
myself of what I was doing anymore. Something that
sounded like my mother's voice kept whispering in the
back of my brain: If you've got it so good, why are you a
junkie? Like I said, I wasn't listening.

We named that unnamed suburban block York
Street, and called our house number one. It was like
some TV dream had come true. I'd bought peace for my
parents. And, by moving to an apartment in Manhattan,
peace for myself.

Susan traveled a lot with me in those days, riding on
the tour buses, seeing and being seen at the best clubs. It
was exciting for us both and great to share together. I
always felt having Susan on my arm lent my act a little
class. And sometimes it really *was* an act. Darin and I
would blow into some place and just take it over. He'd
jump on the stage and drag me up to play guitar while he
sang a mix of his hits, my hits, and the Top Ten Italian
drinking songs.

With her good looks and great personality, Susan was an asset to my career. But that was about as far as it went, I'd try, but I could never really understand how to *be* with a woman, how to stand, and talk . . . how to be friends. Like the young starlets the publicity flacks would arrange as dates for me, Susan was just someone to drape on my arm, looking good when the flashbulbs popped. Sure, we had a past together, but it was the future we were facing now. And, hey, that could change tomorrow.

Look what had already happened. Dion and the Belmonts' second big tour had been booked for early '59. Our latest single, "A Teenager in Love" was rocketing up the charts and into the Top Five. Everything was happening fast. Maybe a little too fast . . .

We'd been billed on a rock 'n' roll extravaganza called the Winter Dance Party, barnstorming the Midwest to ride the wave of "Teenager in Love" as it swept the nation in late 1958. We were going to places we'd never heard of, bringing it to the fans the hard way, one high school auditorium and roller rink at a time. Those long weeks of one-night stands, with only miles of rolling winter badlands in between, did more to change the way I heard music and the way I made it, than anything since Hank Williams. But that wasn't all it changed. The crazy spin on my life was picking up speed. It's hard to make sense of a world where the only rule seems to be "easy come, easy go," when what you want so desperately is just to hold on. So you try to ignore what you can't understand. And that's when it takes you by surprise.

Buddy Holly co-headlined a bill that included Richie Valens, the Big Bopper, and us. Holly had knocked the top of the charts with "That'll Be the Day," come close with "Peggy Sue," and, with his group the Crickets, was headlining the Winter Dance Party on the strength of a new single, "It Doesn't Matter Anymore." We hit it off right away even though, or maybe because, we were from such different worlds. I dug Holly's lean, sparse Texas sound and the way he turned out great music on his own terms. But most of all I admired how together he was.

There wasn't much to do on that tour bus except to make music and try to keep warm. Back then you didn't have the tricked out luxury suites on wheels like stars demand today. We were packed into what looked to me like a converted school bus and, when we got tired, we slept where we were sitting. And when we got tired of that, we'd stretch out in the luggage racks, snoring or just watching our breath in the frigid air. One of the first things that went was the heater. Whenever I hear people talk about the glamour of the rock 'n' roll life, I think of that bus and I have to smile. The new guys—Holly, Richie, the Belmonts and I—didn't know any better. We figured this was how it was always done. But the old-timers—players who'd seen a lot of young talent come and go—definitely knew they were hooked up with a third-class operation.

It was a bitter cold new year with a whole lot of nothing between warm hotel rooms. The bus kept breaking down and it always seemed to happen thirty miles from the nearest town. Like I said, we didn't know enough to be afraid, or what a mid-winter night by the side of the road really meant.

When that bus would wheeze and shudder to a stop, Holly and I used to climb under a blanket together to keep warm. Through the dark hours while we waited for something to happen, we would tell each other stories.

Him, about Lubbock. Me, about the Bronx. I could always get a laugh out of him—soft and low like his drawl—with the one about Pee Wee, running down the street with a red-faced cop behind him.

After a couple of hours, someone would start flagging down cars to drive us to the date. Somehow we managed to keep the tour rolling, town after town, and with it, the music. As the days wore on, I got to know Holly pretty well. Maybe I was always after someone to look up to, but I remember him as being a lot older than me, even though I was nineteen and he was only twenty-two. He was like Darin, someone you respected. Someone that you learned from and modeled yourself after. And one of the things he taught me—and we all taught each other— was music.

It's not hard to understand why we didn't mind the cold. We didn't even think about it. It was tremendously exciting just being around so many guys whose music was so fresh and original. Richie brought that Latin sound of his, filtered through pure rock 'n' roll, and it knocked me out. He'd sit with his feet stretched across the aisle and serenade us in Spanish, all the time playing the meanest rhythm guitar I'd ever heard. The guy was phenomenal. By February, as we were closing in on the Dakotas, that bus was alive with sounds. Buddy's hiccupping rockabilly keyed off our cleanest doo-wop harmonies, mixing to make something brand new. And never heard again.

It was a friendship that lapped over onto the stage. Even though he'd put on six pairs of socks, Holly's drummer came down with frostbitten feet and had to quit the tour. Carlo took over the slot for the rest of the shows. And, of course, we got into some friendly competition. Both Buddy and I had the fanciest guitar on the market, the new Fender Stratocaster: mine, pure white: his, with a sunburst on it. We had a little side bet about who could make his ring the longest. To tell you the truth, I don't remember who won.

Like I said, Buddy was somebody who had his life together. He'd just gotten married and was only at the beginning of a career that had already changed music. You got the feeling he'd made it this far because he knew exactly where he wanted to go. To the top. He was assured and decisive and quick on his feet, and he amazed me because I was always complicating things.

The night before the Fargo, North Dakota, date, he'd worked out a way to get into town early, wash his clothes and get a few hours in a real bed. He'd fly. But he needed some others who would share the charter plane expense and that's what kept me on the bus. It sounded good, but it would cost me $35. That was a month's rent on the old place, a lot of money, I remember thinking. Sure, I was a sophisticated entertainer, a man of the world, but thirty-five bucks was a magic number. It was what needed to be in the cookie jar every month to pay for the roof over our heads.

So, in the end, I decided to stay, to save a buck. Holly rounded up Richie, the Big Bopper, and a pilot, and they went down somewhere in that frozen darkness. We drove all night and when we got to the hotel, instead of familiar faces and familiar jokes, there were only a couple of old people in the lobby watching a flickering TV in silence. The reporter was talking about a plane crash, interviewing an official who said there were no survivors.

I walked back out to the bus and sat alone in the cold. All around me were their belongings, with Buddy's starburst Fender propped against a seat. I don't know how long I was there, and I'm not really sure I thought about anything much. No insight. No grief. No comforting words. I was nineteen years old. Death wasn't real. It was something that happened to old people, who waited out their days in front of the tube.

For $35, one month's rent, my life had been spared. It was the saddest and scariest thing that had ever happened to me, like being let off the hook on a technicality. The death of Buddy and Richie and the rest was like a reminder that no matter how much I thought I was in control, I wasn't. The voice in the back of my brain got a little louder.

CHAPTER 8

The Idolmakers

LAURIE Records' President Alan Sussell had a soft spot in his heart for old standards. We thought it was a soft spot in his head: The last thing the guys and I wanted to do was croon to some old chestnut like "Where or When." But Alan was a beautiful man, a guy we all loved like a father and his favorite song was the old Rodgers and Hart standard. We did the tune on our first LP to show our appreciation for all that Alan had done for us, even though the music was way out of our backyard. It was only the desire to please him that was genuine, so we dutifully gave it our best shot. We opened a new year, and a new decade, with the biggest hit of our career.

Alan, another square in the Schwartz brothers mold, had been right on the money. "Where or When" established Dion and the Belmonts as a national act. Suddenly our pictures were all over the fan magazines and our music all over the radio. We were a sensation, a certified pop music phenomenon, hitting jackpots we'd never even gambled on.

And all the time, behind the scenes, it was steadily coming unraveled, for me and for the group.

Maybe it boiled down to how much stake we all put in making it. For me, it was everything. For Carlo, Freddie, and Angelo, it was different. Suddenly they were a reminder to me of where I'd come from and what I was trying to get away from, of the history I was trying to dump. There was a big, sophisticated world out there and you didn't earn *its* respect with spaghetti stains on your shirt. We'd roll into town and after a show they'd want to go down to the local hangouts, have a few drinks, and break anyone's face that bothered them. The old gang attitude. I had other things on my mind. After all the act was Dion and these other guys. I was the focus, the engine that kept the train rolling. I didn't want anyone to forget that.

But it wasn't just the old ways that were coming between me and the Belmonts. Musically, something else was going down. You could hear it back on that first album, *Presenting Dion and the Belmonts*. The best things, the early things like "I Wonder Why," "Wonderful Girl," "That's My Desire," is pure Bronx soul. That was our music, the reason we'd gotten together in the first place. But our big hit, "A Teenager in Love," with its on-purpose formula, was something else again. We were being pushed into musical directions that had nothing to do with our roots. Instead of a group, we were getting to be a package.

I look back on it now and I laugh. Dion and the Belmonts was such a mix of tragedy and comedy, a real rags-to-riches story down to the details. Sometimes it all seemed like a fast, funny game; one that we were playing by ear.

It's always seemed to me that when a lucky few get into something really good—like the Belmonts and I got into street music—it's usually over for them just when it gets started for everyone else. We were the latest sensation, the newest discovery, but we'd really been around for a long time. At least in the neighborhood. The same with the music. It's the best only when it's sung for pleasure and for free. That was over now, for us, anyway.

As 1960 kicked into high gear, I was too busy getting famous to nurse the monkey on my back full time. Of course, uppers and downers were helping me hit my marks with a smile and a song, but heroin—that seductive, enchanted world all its own—had to wait until I could scrape together a few days off for a weekend binge.

I think even then I knew I needed help, someone to talk to, to help me let loose of it all. I couldn't go to my own dad. He would never understand, so I picked someone else, someone I could respect like a father. One night, after a long recording session, Alan suggested I stay over in a hotel near the studio. We got a room together and started talking. For me the gears had finally started to slip.

It's simple, really, that urge to confess. Just like they used to say at Mount Carmel: It's good for the soul. I'd never really lost the guilt and shame I felt at being a secret junkie. The mother's voice was always there, making me feel I was living a lie, making me crazy, and making the loneliness worse. I was twenty-one years old and there was no way I could understand what was happening to me: the good or the bad. I couldn't separate out who I wanted to be from who I was becoming, and that feeling of losing control was more than I could stand. Which is why I'd sneak back whenever I could into the smothering arms of that white powder, where I could forget about all the contradictions.

Somehow I managed to spill it, or at least some of it, to Alan. Enough, anyway, that he started to see what was going on beneath the slick surface. That same night he got on the phone, making calls until he found out the best hospital around to take care of my problem: The Institute for Living out in Hartford. We were up first thing the next morning, driving up into the lush Connecticut countryside. This is first, Alan said, as we pulled into the gates of this huge, well-tended estate, more like a country club than a hospital. Forget the records, forget the concerts. Forget everything. It'll all be waiting for you when you get back. Just get well.

I'll always be grateful for what Alan tried to do for me, even though the months I spent at that place didn't even begin to scratch the surface of what was really wrong. I got plenty of sleep, ate the best food, and rested secure that this was a joint catering to only the highest class clientele, celebrities like Judy Garland and Bing Crosby. All the greats went through the Institute for Living. I figured I must be doing something right.

It was a kind of enforced vacation and even though my life slowed up a lot, below the calm surface I was still totally out of control. There was a raging blindness inside me, making me walk through walls and over people like they didn't exist. I've never been a tough guy, not even back in the Baldies, but something was driving me to act out all my anger and fear, jerking me around on invisible strings, like one of my dad's puppets. There I was, sitting in a lawn chair in pajamas and slippers, while nurses and attendants made sure I was comfy, learning to play chess with the other "patients," and all the time ready to explode.

I was a victim of all the things I couldn't handle, and that made me want to victimize someone, too. To pass along the pain. One night some aide looked at me the wrong way and before I even knew what I was doing, I decked him with a punch that knocked out a dozen teeth. The guy never had a chance. They took me back to my room and one of the orderlies couldn't help but ask, "Why'd you do that? Why'd you punch out a total stranger?" I honestly didn't know. I honestly didn't want to know. I was hurting, and that pain was changing who I was and how I saw the world. I'd call it a case of Dr. Jekyll and Mr. Hyde, but it wasn't that simple. Both the good guy and the monster were all wrapped up together, like wrestlers on a mat. No one was winning, no one losing: I was paralyzed.

I had a record aimed straight for the top of the charts and every week Alan would send me over the latest fan magazines, usually with my face on the cover, in gorgeous color. My "recuperation" was a total secret, a cover-up for the sake of my image. Publicists kept the fires stoked, our hit kept the kids wanting more. The machine just kept on rolling.

Weeks passed in a kind of haze before the guys in the white coats finally pronounced me cured. I walked out of the institute clean for the first time in years. Inside of a week I was polluted again, making up for lost time and back into the whirlwind that was waiting for me, just like Alan said. Nothing had changed except some part of me deep inside that maybe grew a little colder, a little more alone.

And that was fine by me. I was the only one that was going to straighten out my world, I decided. And only when I was good and ready. Right now it was first things first. And the first thing was my career.

It's easy in hindsight to read between the notes into what was really happening with the group. The Belmonts and I had been together day and night for almost a year and even though I spent a lot of time with them, we weren't really close. It was easy to overlook friendship on the road to stardom, and I drifted further from them as we began to sense just how far we could go. And just what was holding us back.

It was time for me to step out on my own. Leaving the group would be no big legal hassle. When I'd first brought them off the streets I had them signed to a contract separate from mine. We were all free and clear.

Well, sort of. No matter how professional we thought we'd become, there were ties between us stretching back to the neighborhood. I knew how good they really were and had come to count on their polish. They contributed so much, both to what we sounded like and the impact we had on our fans. I was feeling pretty good about myself, sure, but not so good that I could overlook all the talent wrapped up in those three guys. The way they could slide into harmonies like slipping into a custom tailored suit—their input, their support. It was scary to think about leaving all that behind. Yet I knew we were going in different directions. And there were lots of other people around telling me the same thing. All of them very persuasive.

Ever since my days on the bus with Darin I'd had my eye open for a manager who met the qualifications he'd laid down—young, ambitious, a scrapper. Sal

Bonefetti fit the bill. A Brooklyn boy with a lot of music business experience for a guy his age, Sal was only too anxious to manage someone as clearly tagged for the top as me. I liked Sal, his Italian street smarts and hustler's edge, but more important, I believed him when he told me I'd just gotten a taste of what real stardom was like. To jump to the next rung would take a lot of self-confidence and what I didn't have, he'd supply. Look at yourself, he'd tell me; look at your ability. You've got something to offer. He tried to motivate me and even while I was smiling and nodding I wondered if I was blowing a good thing.

I'd become so dependent on what the people around me said I should do, said was good for me, that I had no idea what *I* wanted to do. Sal threw down a challenge, even while he tried to convince me I had what it took. He was doing what most good managers should be able to do—stroke their client's ego to get out the best performance. After all, it was in both our interests.

But at the same time, Sal wasn't telling me anything I hadn't already thought of myself. For one thing, it was getting clearer with each recording session that the group and I just weren't on the same track. Ever since the Holly tour, I'd felt an itch to move away from the smooth harmonies that connected our music to its doo-wop roots and, instead, get into the fast-changing world of rock 'n' roll. For a long time we'd been trying to mix the two and it just wasn't working out. They were forever loyal to the Five Satins and the Four Aces and all I wanted to do was let my Fender ring all night. "Where or When" turned out to be our swan song, the last time Carlo, Angelo, Freddie, and I ever put our voices together and came up golden. As the golden glow of the Fifties faded, Dion and the Belmonts called it quits.

The early Sixties was a strange time for music, with upstanding citizens still shaking their fingers and wagging their tongues over the immoral jungle rhythms that were seducing their kids. No one in the recording business knew how long rock 'n' roll would last. Or how long it would be allowed to last. So they were constantly trying to fit the sound into the safer, more legitimate world of what they called "good music." Of course, they couldn't do a thing with a lot of the most popular rock 'n' roll performers. Little Richard and Jerry Lee Lewis weren't going to appeal to the supper club crowd no matter how many candelabras you put on their piano tops. But there were other guys, guys like Darin and Anka and me, that they were trying to push into a tuxedo mold, like junior league Sinatras and Bennetts. Some of us, like Darin especially, could move in and out of either scene. Others, like Frankie Avalon and Bobby Rydell, got stuck doing drippy music calculated to placate the old folks. It was like a counterfeit of the real thing, a way to tap into some of the popularity, and profits, of teenage music without any of the danger.

Then there was me. I think if I'd known who I was and what I wanted, if I hadn't started losing touch with why I'd become a singer in the first place, I might have found the courage to run my own career. To tell the handlers and molders and inside operators what they could do for me and not the other way around. But it wasn't that simple; after a while it gets so you can't remember the sound of your own voice, because all you're hearing is everyone else's. You don't want to miss the mark they've all set, so you try to become part of the team. You figure at least these guys know; after all, they've brought you this far. They press records and book concerts and sit at desks behind autographed pictures of stars. They're a part of what you're trying to get into. But you're never quite sure of what belongs to them and what you get to keep for yourself.

The success of "Where or When" gave Laurie Records the green light for more of the same. The Belmonts and I had started cutting an album called *When You Wish Upon A Star,* which was nothing but standards. I didn't dig it. But the Belmonts really seemed to enjoy the opportunity to dish up some more smooth harmonies. It was the beginning of some real friction between me and the guys.

Part of the problem was that all I could really do was fake that full-blown lounge singer style. It was easier for the Belmonts to get into redoing things like "In the Still of the Night"; the harmonies weren't that much different from our old stuff, just the feeling. But I was never that kind of vocalist. I didn't have the pipes for it. What I didn't know then is clear enough now; my gift isn't in hitting and holding notes, it's in communicating what a song is all about. That's what I'd learned from Hank and Holly and all the rest. I could deliver a song, but I wasn't just a showman. I was a storyteller.

Laurie released a couple more singles from those sessions, including our version of "When You Wish Upon A Star." It made the Top Forty, but by that time the group was history. I think it was hard for Angelo, Freddie, and Carlo when the joy ride was over and suddenly they were just three guys looking for a reason to stay together. But I was too caught up to notice. It was like someone had thrown open the throttle and all I could do

was hang on for dear life. Sal, Alan, Gene Schwartz—
they were all gearing up for the big push and it was up to
me to make the grade or disappoint a lot of people. Dis-
appointing people was something I couldn't stand to do.

I was pretty impressed with myself. I'd made a million twice over by the time I was twenty-one. I'd been on
"The Ed Sullivan Show" singing standards, maybe, but
that was my mug in America's living rooms. I'd bought
my parents a home and could give my girl the best time
in New York City. If I went to a party, I'd be the center
of attention, with beautiful people asking me to tell them
all about myself. I was in front of audiences all the time
and their applause was still my drug of choice. Sure, I
was shooting smack, more than ever, but the real narcotic
was all the adulation. I believed it all. I needed it all.

And all I was doing was working overtime to fill the
void, that dark place where all the uncertainty, the guilt
and doubt, had taken root. I thought if I could just get
enough money, fame, and recognition, things would finally start to make sense. Instead, the more success I got,
the tighter the chains felt.

"Lonely Teenager" was my first solo release and it
reached number fourteen on the charts. Not too shabby
for my first time out, I figured. Neither did Sal, who set
me up with a schedule that made the Belmont days look
like a holiday at Jones Beach. One tour blended into another across the next couple of years, and whether I liked
it or not my career came first. Most of the time I was too
tired to care. I was earning big money, bigger than ever,
playing anywhere the price was right. It was a strange
mix of gigs. I was still straddling the rock 'n' roll fence,
half the time belting out my hits in front of screaming,
dancing teenagers, the other half crooning standards to

folks with blue hair at places that reminded me a little too much of the venues my dad used to play.

My musical split personality was summed up best, I think, on my first solo album, *Alone with Dion*. There I was on the cover in all my smoky Latin glory, wearing a silk ascot with some babe in chartreuse gloves wrapping her arms around me. Inside the gatefold, with all the fan club snaps, was a message from Gene: "This album represents the fulfillment of a longstanding ambition of Dion's to record material that he feels is best suited to express himself as an artist. . . ."

If you believe that one I've got a bridge you might be interested in. Remakes of "Fools Rush In" and "One For My Baby" were hardly my idea of "expressing myself as an artist." A couple of numbers from Doc and Morty, "Save the Last Dance for Me" and "Havin' Fun" were more like it, but nowhere on that album could you hear the edge and excitement I wanted to bring to my music. I was playing their game, by their rules.

I guess even more revealing is the note I penned for that inside cover. "When I started to record this album," I wrote, "I looked up into the control booth and saw some of my friends: my manager, the men behind Laurie. They were all there to say they believed in me." They were in the control booth all right, and what they believed in was their ability to mold me into their image of a suave, successful pretender to Sinatra's throne.

Needless to say, I preferred rock 'n' roll. In mid-1961 I went out on another all-black tour, this time with Little Willie John and Bobby Blue Bland headlining. Man, I really dug Bobby's action. He hired a guy to comb his hair, another one to do his nails. Everything about the guy was an acknowledgment that, yes, it was good to be a star. Very good, indeed.

Johnny Mathis thought so, too, although sometimes it seemed to me he was dreaming the whole thing. I shared a few dates with him around that time, and after the show we'd sometimes go out to get a bite to eat. I'd sit at a table with him and want to wave my hand in front of his face: "Hello? Anybody home?" Johnny was where I wanted to be, with three years worth of giant hits already racked up, but while all that fame and adulation got my blood pumping, it only seemed to daze him. Being around Mathis was like looking at a guy through the wrong end of a telescope.

Del Shannon, on the other hand, was a real live wire. He'd just rocketed to the top with "Runaway" and was one of the most exciting guitarists I'd heard since Richie Valens. He was also a great songwriter. On one tour with Del we got to talking about how to write hit songs. We each had a theory: Del said you had to get girls feeling sorry for you, make them want to lay your head on their shoulder. He did "Hats Off to Larry" to prove it. Wrong, I'd say. You've got to put them down. And I wrote "Runaround Sue" to prove it. It was the winter of 1961 and I had my first number one hit.

I'd done a couple of stiff singles between "Lonely Teenager" and "Runaround Sue"—throwaway tunes like "Kissin' Game," which convinced me that what Sal was saying was true: The big time doesn't always come easy. "Runaround Sue" was different and in a way it proved what I'd been feeling all along, but never had the nerve to say. I really was at my best when I rocked. Most everything else I was cutting at that point was a formula, calculated to pick up on some other singer's sound. Morty and Doc, for instance, had tried to follow-up on Ricky Nelson's "Poor Little Fool" when they wrote "A Teenager in Love." And the inspiration for "Runaround Sue" came from some after-hours song swapping I'd done with Gary U.S. Bonds, riding high at the time with "New Orleans."

I wrote "Sue" with a young songwriter named Ernie Maresca, who was behind some of my other big hits. A guy who enjoyed a few cocktails, Ernie summed up his whole philosophy with one phrase, said a million times: "Strange world, eh D?" Luckily he was a lot better with songs. From the opening bars, "Runaround Sue" was right in there. The backing singers were a Brooklyn group called the Del Satins with a sound as smooth as their name, and the arrangement made the most of a cooking tempo. I've always felt really good about "Sue." She got me to the top and did it with a little style.

Style, after all, was what it was all about. Style, and money and mobs of people who just wanted to touch the hem of my custom-tailored threads. It *was* a strange world, glittery and jittery and happening so fast, the best moments were becoming nothing but a blur. Sure, I was lost, alone, and hurting. But they just kept telling me I'd never had it so good. Who was I to argue?

CHAPTER 9

The Wanderer

LATER —much later —when I finally got a handle on those crazy, top heavy years, I caught a glimpse of what really went on while I was staring at my reflection in a gilt-edged mirror. The shock of that sudden understanding caught me up short. Until that moment it all seemed like an accident, some coincidence or trick of fate, that I'd survived at all. It's like riding on bald tires down a bad road through a rainstorm. You run a red light and suddenly you're into a skid. You hit the brakes, you turn the wheel, but that sickening slide hurtles you toward the guard rail, and the cliff on the other side. You know you're gonna die, you know you deserve to die, but just then the car lurches to a stop, inches from oblivion. Somebody up there likes you.

Even while I was throwing away everything that was real and true and good in my life, even at the lowest ebb of anger and despair, there were angels standing guard round me. And I don't mean the ones with harps and wings. I guess I'm like anyone else when it comes to taking the treasures of life for granted; we never notice them until they're gone. Or driven away. But somebody up there really *does* like us and that changes everything. At least it does for me. The best things are the simple things and the simple things are the hardest to get—peace with yourself, the love of your wife, a family for your old age. For some of us, being happy, and whole, ain't easy. We need all the help we can get.

Was Susan an angel sent to help me through? It's seemed that way from time to time, but she's really just like the rest of us, I guess, looking to be happy and whole. The miracle is that she was always there for me. No matter what it cost her. That was tough sometimes, really tough. She didn't take a walk on me, even though there were times maybe she should've. I know I would've. Maybe it seems like she should have stood up for herself, cut her losses, and saved her dignity. Maybe. All I know is that she loved me when I didn't know what love was, how to give or receive it. She loved me when it cost her something. Like I said, we may take them for granted, but miracles happen every day.

No, "Runaround Sue" *wasn't* about Susan. At least, Susan wasn't the one running around. She'd moved into an east side apartment with three girlfriends, including my publicist Connie DeNave, the one who'd put together the purple glove bit for the cover of *Alone with Dion*. Susan was working days and making the Manhattan club scene with me at night, coming out on tours whenever she could get the time off. It was an exciting life and Susan really blossomed in the glare of the high life. With her flaming hair and great wardrobe, she could keep up with the best of them. She knew how to be liked by just being herself. That part came easy. I was the one giving her trouble.

All kinds of things start falling your way when you reach the top. All kinds of opportunities, interesting and irresistible. And by late 1961, opportunity wasn't just knocking, it was pounding down the door. The follow-up to "Runaround Sue" was another Ernie Maresca original called "The Wanderer." By December it had peaked at number two, one shy of "Sue." Not that it really mattered. The handlers were happy. Even the flip side, a swinging dance thing called "The Majestic" was a hit. I was happy, too. "The Wanderer" rocked.

With the drums way out front and Buddy Lucas's sizzling sax break, "The Wanderer" was the hippest thing I'd done to date. I *swaggered* through the tune, putting a little growl into it, relishing Ernie's great macho lyrics and boosted again by the Del Satins smooth backing vocals. With a driving rhythm and a clean arrangement, the song caught hold instantly. "That's more like it," was the feeling I had.

Susan and I dropped by the neighborhood shortly after "The Wanderer" hit the streets to see Ricky and I'll never forget the response I got from old friends. The tune hit a common chord, capturing some of the excitement of the real street music we could all remember. It had become like the theme song of Crotona Avenue. No question about it, I was on a roll.

With two major hits to my name, offers to put it up on a marquee came hot and heavy. Of course, movie roles were just another way to sanitize rock 'n' rollers, a tried and true tactic since Elvis. And the movies they gave us to act in were usually as silly as the songs they wanted us to sing. But who cared? No one ever heard of things like "oversaturation" and "media burnout" back then. You got as much mileage as you could from what might just be a flash in the pan. Like records and concerts, movies were another way of running with the money.

The first feature Sal landed for me was a thing called *Ten Girls Ago,* a B-movie comedy with a plot that's best left forgotten. It starred three of the greatest comics working then, Buster Keaton, Bert Lahr, and Eddie Foy, Jr. Keaton, of course, was a silent comedy genius, and Lahr had played the Cowardly Lion in *The Wizard of Oz.* Foy had been popular since the golden days of radio. The love interest was me and a young actress named Jennifer Billingsley. Shooting called for three months of locations in Toronto.

I'd dated other starlets, the young Ann-Margret, for instance, hanging out at the Copa or Jack Silverman's International, where I performed, waiting to get our pictures snapped. It was all for the publicity. But Jennifer was different. When we were first introduced, she was the lead dancer in the Broadway production of *Carnival*—very talented, very beautiful, and troubled. In the weeks before and during the *Ten Girls Ago* shoot we spent a lot of time together. I was fascinated with her—with her free spirit and unpredictability. We were a lot alike, I think, in the way we were handling fame. She'd been picked out of flocks of starlets and groomed for the big time, and, like me, woke up one morning and couldn't find herself.

Not that I was looking for mental stimulation, but Jennifer was bright and sophisticated and poised. What really drew me to her like a magnet, though, was that edgy feeling of danger she carried with her, like a time bomb ticking the seconds away. I guess the sound of our two clocks just meshed.

Things might have gone further than they did if I hadn't realized that Jennifer was carrying around a load of pain all her own. She'd come from a horrendous background that caught her and held her in a web even stronger than mine. Just being around her was like losing control, a temporary insanity that left me drained and a little frightened. She was headstrong, flighty, and desperate. And for a while I dug it like a moth digs a flame.

For me faithfulness, like everything else, was a matter of opinion. Susan was my girl, I never doubted that, but I never checked to see how she felt about it either. Why should I? One of the funny things about being a star is that, instead of more freedom, you get less. If you want them to, there's always someone else around to make the right decisions for you, so you start to forget what it's like to take the initiative. In anything. For going on six years, Susan and I had had an "understanding" that one day . . . maybe. Marriage was a choice too big for me to make and Susan wouldn't do it for me. With Jennifer I didn't have to decide. She was like a mysterious mix of pain and pleasure that I knew couldn't last. It was a fling: a word that kind of summed up both our lives.

I was picking up a lot on the set of that dumb little movie, and not just tips about method acting. Buster, Bert, and Eddie were guys who'd been in the business longer than I'd been alive, and they did what they did like it was second nature. They didn't work at being funny, polishing their timing and delivery. It was all instinct with them, honed and perfected on a thousand vaudeville stages. Every day for months I'd ride out to locations with them, waiting for one of them to set the others off and then laughed so hard my sides ached. Most of their best stuff was show biz shticks way over my head. Not that it mattered. Their mastery of storytelling, hitting just the right details to keep you going, was what amazed me. Of course, they were also able to pull it off in front of a camera. Watching Keaton work was like seeing some acrobat balanced on a high wire. His precision was awesome. At one point the script called for him to get knocked down by a waist-high swinging door six times in as many different ways. It took several takes to get it down and each time Buster made the fall exactly at the right moment, landing exactly in the right spots and getting exactly the same laughs from the cast and crew.

Then there was the day Buster and I were killing time shooting a little pool—nine ball. I was showing off. When it was his turn to shoot, he ambled up to the table and said, "I'm gonna clean up." He grabbed a broom, swept all the balls off the table and ran out of the room. Just like that.

Not long after, an insurance man came by the set, trying to peddle an insurance policy to Bert Lahr. "Insurance?" he said. "I don't even buy green bananas."

When we were together on the screen they'd have to constantly cut and tell these veterans to stop upstaging everyone else. "Give the kids a break!" the director would shout. It was what being a pro was all about.

So was the terrible fear of being over the hill. As good as they were, and with all the years of people telling them so, I'd never met three more insecure guys in my life. I started thinking that maybe my dad was the lucky one: He'd never made it anywhere near the top. They had and it was so high up they were terrified of looking down. Before any big scene, for instance, one of them would always knock on my trailer door wondering what pair of shoes to wear, how to read a line, or which side of his face looked best. Sometimes, before they'd go on camera, they'd duck behind the set and throw up. I'd like to think that something inside me clicked when I saw that; something that said, "See? No matter how much you get, you're never sure" But, to tell you the truth, I don't remember hearing it.

So, you're probably asking yourself, if *Ten Girls Ago* was such a big career break, how come I've never heard of it? Funny about that. See, part of that unmentionable plot revolved around these three dogs—a collie, a dachshund, and a sheep dog—in a love triangle. At least I think that's what it was about. Anyway, these dogs were in practically every scene and it wasn't until the picture was three quarters done that some bright guy noticed that the girl dog the other two were after wasn't a girl at all. You wouldn't think they'd overlook something that obvious, but there it was and the only thing to do was shoot it all over again.

Get yourself another boy, was what Sal said and told me to pack my bags. I was due out on the road again, to promote my new album *Runaround Sue*.

While I was in the studio recording the title track I played around with two tympani drums left over from a classical music session. The drums still had their canvas covers over them, but I kept them on because it created just the sort of muffled thud I was after. It was that kind of spontaneity that could still make music fun.

Musically, I was more in the pocket than ever before and the twelve cuts on that album proved it. Aside from the hits, I'd included my version of Darin's "Dream Lover," and a great roadhouse rendition of "Kansas

City." Ernie and I put together a thing called "Lonely World," one of our better efforts, and I put a good spin on Goffin and King's "Take Good Care of My Baby."

Carole and Gerry were two more songwriters I liked hanging out with. Same with Cynthia Weil and Barry Mann. I knew that being a good performer was half talent, half luck. Writing good songs was another matter entirely. That was talent plus hard work and I had a lot of admiration for people who could make it big and not let it go to their heads. They were professionals, all right, but they stayed the same no matter how many hits they had on the charts. They were relaxed and consistent, writing songs because they loved it. Not because they had something to prove.

"The Wanderer," on the other hand, had proved I could get hits with real rock 'n' roll and Sal wasn't about to buck the trend. I was doing stuff I could sink my teeth into and connecting with the kids. "Runaround Sue" and "The Wanderer" were both big with college kids and I found myself doing fewer blue hair specials and hitting more campuses.

And what I was getting down in the studio was coming across on stage. Sal would book me on a string of one-nighters down South, in the Midwest, or along the eastern seaboard, and I'd go out for three or four weeks straight, hitting one sold-out auditorium after another, usually as a headliner. I'd hire a band, the best guys out of New York or Chicago, and front the whole show wearing my Stratocaster with the amp cranked as high as I could get it. I'd bring down the house and it wouldn't be with "When You Wish upon a Star." I was aiming a lot higher.

And scoring every time. Nineteen sixty-two was

turning out to be a huge year with three consecutive Top Ten singles. "Lovers Who Wander," courtesy of Ernie and me, was a handclapper in the "Sue" mold, and by the spring of that year it had charged up to number three. I followed it with my first original ever to make the charts. "Little Diane" was a combination of both me and Del's songwriting approach—I was putting them down *and* making them feel sorry for me at the same time.

Pelham Bay, across from the Bronx Zoo, was a Jewish neighborhood back then. I was passing by a synagogue one day when I heard some of the music leaking out. It was different from anything I knew about so I went inside. I dug what I was hearing so much I ended up making friends with the cantor, a guy named Henry Rosenblatt. He took me into the back and played me records of his dad, who was in the original *Jazz Singer*. The music was unique, and soulful, and when I wrote "Little Diane," I was picking up on the style of the great Cantor Rosenblatt.

Both tunes ended up on my third solo album, *Lovers Who Wander,* which picked up right from where *Runaround Sue* left off. And then some. I was knocking back some of my best work, singing at peaks that I didn't know I could reach, pushing up the drum sound, jumping right into the middle of some cooking arrangements with both feet and staying one step ahead of the trends.

What really got me going was the chance to sing my own music. I covered Lloyd Price's "Stagger Lee" and the Isley Brothers' rave-up "Shout," but I was also doing originals like "(I Was) Born to Cry" and "Sandy." The first was a bona fide blues number, with a "Saint James Infirmary" feel that took self-pity to new heights. The second was an up-tempo pop workout, which bounced along on some doo-wopish scat singing. I gave both of them everything I had.

By the time the snow was on the ground that year I was back on top again with another original, "Love Came To Me," and Sal was starting to lay out the groundwork for the next big phase of my career. Part of his plan called for a jump to Columbia Records, where better promotion and distribution would pump sales way over their levels at Laurie. Gene, Bob, and Alan had been with me since the beginning, but even they couldn't deny that the stakes had suddenly gotten a lot higher. I wasn't the kid from Crotona Avenue anymore. I was a hot commodity, a major meal ticket, and it was only a matter of time before the scent of money wafted uptown.

That was the music business; not so different, I guess, from any other line of work that sometimes forces you to make a choice between friends and a career. But like I said, I wasn't the one making the decisions, or taking the responsibility. I was getting real good at just leaving things up to my manager, my agent, my producer, or whoever else was on the payroll.

Another part of Sal's strategy was to pick up on my popularity overseas. He arranged a big tour of South America to test the waters for a later European swing. "The closest I've come to a 'steady' is my career," they had me write on the liner notes of *Runaround Sue*: "She's a pretty demanding chick. But in a couple of years, who knows?" I think I might even have believed it myself. I was in for a rude awakening.

CHAPTER 10

Montevideo

AS fast as my career was changing, inside I was changing even faster—changes I couldn't control, couldn't even keep up with. I was becoming a different person, one that was getting used to a good life in the fast lane. But even as the Bronx duckling was turning into the suave swan, he was clinging to the last shreds of his old life, with all its familiar patterns.

Take money. I had enough to do pretty much what I wanted, but when it comes right down to it, you can run out of reasons to blow bread real quick. It must have been my mother's influence—that and memories of endlessly trying to make short ends meet—but I was never really good at letting money slip through my fingers.

Even at the height of my popularity, I lived under my means. I had a good apartment, a great wardrobe, and a car; I didn't need twelve more of the same. Everything I owned I paid for outright. I wanted it to be mine, not the bank's or anyone else who could take it away. I made sure my sisters and parents were provided for—that everybody looked good when I took them out for a night on the town—but once that was taken care of I didn't see the point of throwing cash around just to dazzle the masses. For me, $35 was still a month's rent.

Which meant I could have lived for years on what I drank, swallowed, and shot away. Drugs were the one big exception to my frugal habits and I thought nothing of dropping a couple of big bills to beef up my stash. I squandered thousands on my habits without a thought. Clothes and cars were great to have, but smack . . . that was a necessity.

No, the changes that were happening to me were inside, deep inside, where your personality can get twisted and bent like so much taffy. I felt like I was getting smarter and smoother and more hip to what the world was all about. Actually, the pressure of that world was turning me into a stranger—someone I didn't even know, and wouldn't have liked if I had.

My mother used to say I was a wonderful kid. Up until the age of twelve. After that, I changed. Maybe so. But those changes were nothing compared to what I was going through now. You can measure someone's age by how cynical and disillusioned they are, charting that distance between the dreams they start out with and the compromises they settle for. Sometimes you can even lick the odds, when you're too young to know it can't be done. But when you do find out the truth you've got two choices—accept the inevitable or cling to the dream. Or, somewhere between the two, maybe find a measure of peace within yourself . . . with who you are, your limitations and potential.

For me, it was different. There was no limit to how high I could go. The wild blue yonder was the ceiling of my success, as long as I kept on my toes and could leave the competition in the dust. By the same token, there was no basement too low for me to call home. I'd already been faced with the grim reality of the secret darkness in my soul when I tried getting clean at the institute. It would take a lot more than an expensive stay in the country to straighten out what was coiled up in my gut. Mine was a world of no compromise, a Technicolor epic on a cinerama screen. My dreams were coming true like clockwork. So were my nightmares.

What was wrong? Nothing, I'd tell myself over and over, trying to blot out the whispering fears. Any problems here? Not a thing, I insisted, turning to the next record, the next gig, the next hit, hoping, always hoping, that happiness was waiting on the pinnacle. What was that gnawing feeling that wouldn't go away? Must have been something I ate.

Somehow it always seemed that my life was *about* to happen: I was never really living it, just waiting for the curtain to rise and the show to get on the road. I felt like a kid who's found all his Christmas presents stashed on the top shelf of his folks' closet. He knows they're all gonna be his, but the surprise and pleasure is gone. Only the guilt hangs on. Good things kept coming my way, but I didn't deserve them. Somehow I was getting cheated.

It was also getting to where the tension was too much to bear. If money, fame, and drugs weren't getting me over, what would? It was a question that hung in the air like a bad smell. I needed distraction, entertainment. I needed witty, beautiful, adoring people around me all the time. I'd changed all right; from that kid who could amuse himself with a song for hours to a guy who couldn't stand his own company for more than five minutes.

My apartment, in a ritzy building on Sixty-third

Street, was like a *House Beautiful* spread. All the latest
furniture, breathtaking view, spotless and clean and new.
Part of the reason was that I was hardly ever there to
mess things up. After an evening club-hopping or coming
off the road, I'd crash for a few hours, get up, and feel
like I'd landed in jail. If I sat down, it would be on the
edge of the seat, tapping my feet and drumming my fingers. Most of the time, though, I was pacing, talking on
the phone, trying to round up someone to come over and
talk or get high with me. If it was six in the morning or
three at night, it didn't matter. I needed people around
and if I couldn't find anyone I'd jump in the car and race
up to Westchester to hang out with my family.

Not that it helped. All I could ever seem to get from
them was some left-handed compliments and a lot of advice about how I was blowing my career by not singing
like Sinatra or combing my hair like Anka. They were
good at stoking the fire of my insecurity, always had
been. I never got over the feeling of having to give them
a report whenever I saw them, running down all my
latest triumphs, looking in vain for some kind of pat on
the back and ending up with two fistfuls of resentment.
Nothing I ever did was good enough. It's an old com-
plaint, I guess, common to kids everywhere. After a
while, they tell me, you're supposed to give up trying and
find that approval in yourself. But I never learned how to
do that. I was hung up back in a railroad flat at 749 East
183rd Street, trying to fix things up. Trying to make it
nice.

"This is my life!" I sometimes wanted to scream. Let
me do it my way. They had no idea what it was like,
always having to top yourself and then turning around to
try and live up to some impossible ideal they had about

you. I was getting from my parents the same messages I picked up everywhere else: You're only as good as your last record. What have you done for us lately? Don't look behind you, someone might be gaining.

The fantasy world of fame, my isolation, and a wheelbarrow full of other people's expectations—it was all starting to reach down into my core, blunting the edges and blurring the outlines. It wasn't just my desire to win. It was my obsession not to lose. I guess I knew that if the house of cards ever blew down, I'd tumble with it. There was nothing propping me up but the flattery of strangers.

Things came to a head during that barnstorming tour of South America late in 1962. I'd been out of the country before with Roy Orbison in Australia, but it was nothing like being thrown into places where even the air smelled different. I was desperate, searching for something familiar.

Only there was no escape. I couldn't hop in the car and drive from Buenos Aires to White Plains for a dose of home cooking. I didn't know the language. How was I going to find someone to talk to? I couldn't even get high. How do you ask a Venezuelan busboy for a nickel bag? The whole three weeks was one sold-out hall after another, mad dashes for the limo, the next plane, the next photo opportunity and then, the sudden crushing loneliness in a hotel room along some empty boulevard in town where summer came in December. It was all getting old, fast. And I finally hit bottom in Montevideo, Uruguay.

Sal had hung in for the first week of the tour before heading back to the states to wrap up the Columbia deal. I'd been alone with a million foreigners ever since, and by the time the tour stormed into Montevideo I felt like a punching bag with all the air let out. It's probably a real nice burg, Montevideo, with lots of statues of guys on horseback and come-hither señoritas sipping espresso at sidewalk cafes. Probably. To tell you the truth, all I remember about the place was the dripping faucet in my luxury suite. It was like one of those timers on a game show, ticking out the last few seconds before they send you home with the consolation prize. I had time—nothing but time—and nothing to do with it but think. And listen. That mother's voice was loud and clear now, scolding me, rubbing my nose in the misery I felt, giving me a stern talking-to for my own good.

Sometimes guilt gets to haunting you so much you forget how to say you're sorry. It feeds on itself—that feeling of being busted, tried, and convicted of everything you've ever done or fallen short of doing—and there's no reprieve. No second chance. You want to change, you'd do anything to do the right thing, but it's already too late. Saying you're sorry, wanting to begin again . . . it all seems so pathetic. You'll never change, that voice keeps telling you, so what's the point of saying you're sorry, that you'll do better next time? Who do you think you're kidding?

What was missing for me, what I never knew I could have and hold, was the ability to forgive myself and others. All the pain and disappointment and anger: I could never let it go, never let it slide. There were so many debts that needed to be paid—people that owed me and people I owed—that it just never occurred to me to take the loss and move on. Of all the things in my life that weren't there, forgiveness left the biggest hole. I was bound up in guilt with that voice in my head like a doomsday bell, telling me I'd made my bed, now sleep in it. If I could.

But I couldn't. Sleep, like forgiveness, wouldn't come, and the nights I spent in Montevideo, tossing and turning in a confusion that was churning me like butter, felt like they would never end. But they always do, even down there under the Equator, where everything is upside down. Dawn would come and the fishwives and fruit vendors would start hocking their wares, just like back on Crotona Avenue and I'd get up, wash my face and take a long, slow shave. There was a brand-new day waiting to be faced.

What I'd finally gotten hip to, halfway across the world, was that I couldn't face it alone. You may be a Ph.D., but the day you get smart is the day you realize it's all too much for one guy to whip. Montevideo was like looking into a crystal ball and seeing the worst future imaginable; one where nothing was ever different. I was twenty-three years old. Would I still be doing this— sitting alone in silent hotel rooms—when I was fifty? You're born. You spend the first half getting up to speed, the second half running down. Then they say some nice words over you. I was a pop star. I might last a while longer, fading in the pages of someone's teenage scrap book, but that didn't change the end of the story.

Hey, it happens to the best of us. We get older, in spite of our best efforts. I wanted something stable for myself. Naturally I turned to Susan. She was the one constant in my life, a link to the past and, now, a bridge to some new future, brighter and more hopeful. As soon as I got home, I promised myself, I'd ask her to marry me.

She'd be thrilled, right? On the long plane ride back,

with the memory of Montevideo falling away through the clouds, I started feeling pretty good about myself again. After all, didn't all the magazines pick me as their most eligible catch? Nineteen sixty-three was just around the corner—another year, another peak. I was an egomaniac with an inferiority complex. One terrific guy.

And now I had another reason to feel good: The Columbia deal had closed. Five years for a half million dollars. It was a lot of money for the time and more than most from the neighborhood had ever made. In their lives. Susan was one lucky girl.

I know Susan loves me, but I've never quite been able to figure out why she married me. She's a level-headed woman—it's her best trait—with a cool appraising eye. And, believe me, the whole time she was weighing the odds. I found that out years later when Ricky asked us why we'd been married in a Unitarian church. It was Sal, I explained. He told me that the Unitarians believed in a one-for-all and all-for-one God and I'd like the sound of that. Wrong, said Susan. "The reason we got married in a Unitarian church was that I knew Dion was crazy, and had a lot of problems. I loved him, but I figured if it didn't work out, we wouldn't have to get a divorce because we hadn't been married in a real church." Like I said, levelheaded.

Susan and I tied the knot March 25, 1963. Jack, her dad, didn't have a lot of cash but insisted on paying for the wedding. I had five hundred relatives on my side; she had two, including a lone aunt. We ended up just inviting the heads of the various branches of the DiMucci clan. My dad was best man. Ricky was there. So were Susan's roommates. And the press. It felt funny, standing at that altar, like both a new beginning and an overdue finale.

Something long unspoken had finally been acknowledged: We were meant for each other.

But I was sweating under the collar that balmy spring day and not just from bridegroom jitters. I was shaky from relief. Stepping off the South American express I thought I was sitting pretty, with my marriage proposal ready and my future assured. It was right about then that she knocked me off my perch.

Just like I'd hung around with older cats when I first got into the business, so younger singers were starting to hang around me, picking up tips and a little luster. It gave me a charge and some of the guys I really liked. Like Tony Orlando. There was something real about Tony, a gentleness that had helped him to overcome some real hardship in his life. At that time he was supporting his disabled sister and he had one foot on the ladder I'd just climbed. We'd hang out together when I was in town and, once in a while, Susan would come along.

When I heard that Susan and Tony had gone out a few times together while I was south of the border, I think I must have broken out in a cold sweat that didn't quit until we'd said "I do." I didn't stop to ask if she was doing it just to wake me up or if this sweet, good-looking kid was a serious thing. I didn't care. Suddenly all the air went out of my balloon. I was ready to beg.

I didn't have to. The truth was, behind all the bluster and hedged bets, we really needed each other. That hadn't changed since that day in front of Crazy Tony's. All we did under the eyes of an all-for-one God was let what was meant to be happen.

A copy of the original poster from the last show that Buddy Holly, Ritchie Valens, and the Big Bopper ever played together

Singing my new song "Teenager in Love" to Buddy Holly. It was the last time I ever saw him.

In my silver-and-black T-Bird, out for some
White Castle hamburgers

I moved to Manhattan but I'm still up on
the roof.

Rama

Doing my thing on "The Ed Sullivan Show"—*in a tux,* 1961

With the president of Columbia Records, Goddard Lieberson. I was the first rock 'n' roller to sign with CBS; it was 1963.

With Buster Keaton, a frustrated rock 'n' roller, on the set of our movie "Ten Girls Ago," 1962

On the same set with Bert Lahr—what stories he had to tell!

I took this picture of Susan—you can see why I fell so deeply in love.

Our wedding day in March 1963—the best thing that ever happened to me

Susan at our home on the Hudson River, with Mojo, 1965

**Singing some Bronx blues at the Bitter
End in Greenwich Village, 1965**

My father-in-law, Jack, 1968

A poster for my record *Abraham, Martin and John*, which sold three million copies in 1968. It has a special meaning for me because it's about four men with a vision.

CHAPTER 11

Columbia

RUBY Baby" was my first single for Columbia Records, a number two song and my fourth consecutive Top Ten hit. I was working with the best now, the biggest record company, the hottest arrangers, the surest thing. Columbia was the top recording label in America, accustomed to starting their new artists with a breakthrough and building from there. I was the first rock 'n' roll artist signed to the label and, naturally, expectations ran high. As Laurie Records' biggest star, I sometimes got the feeling I was carrying the company. There was no question who was on whose shoulders at Columbia.

I liked it that way. If Alan, Bob, Gene, and I were a team, then what Columbia assembled on my behalf was a task force. No expense was spared and no excuses accepted. This was the big time. I was getting $100,000 a year, guaranteed, whether I sold a record or not. But with all that money came the pressure to justify the investment and "Ruby Baby" was a great downpayment. I'd always loved the old Drifters' song; I'd grown up to it. Bob Mersey and I put it into a simple arrangement. It had that effortless groove that was always there in my best stuff. It was all funky acoustic guitar, hand claps, foot stomps, and a strolling bass line that broke into syncopated skips as the tune came round for the finish. "Ruby Baby" was a natural—probably the happiest couple of minutes I've ever done.

But even as it was streaking up the charts in January 1963, I was back taking orders from the movers and shakers. One more rock hit only made them that much more anxious to legitimize me in the "real" music world. No matter how clever or catchy this music was, it was still a gimmick, a fad like hula hoops and slinkys. I wasn't a teenager anymore, they kept telling me; you've got to move on to a more grown up audience. What did I know? They were getting rich out of making me famous. That made them the experts. Experts at what worked, what had always worked. The Columbia execs, guys like Goddard Lieberson, who'd brought me to the label, had helped lay out the blueprints for the modern recording industry and they never gave up trying to steer me down the road they'd paved. And all the while I was struggling to hang on to the joy I once knew from just singing—not for money, not for fame, just for fun. Like some forlorn echo, that feeling was fading quick.

You can hear it happening on the *Ruby Baby* album, my debut long-player for my new label. It was like they were forcing me back into a mold I'd wriggled out of back before my solo days. I was cutting more "mature" music again—chestnuts like "The End of the World," "You Made Me Love You," and "You're Nobody 'Til Somebody Loves You." The arrangements were big and brassy, goosing the tunes with slick tricks of the trade. Mersey pulled out all the stops on those twelve tracks, but, for me, it was just more of the same. Worse, I was trying to write tunes that would appeal to my parents, not my friends. Most of the stuff I'd put together for the album was co-written with a Tin Pan Alley veteran named Noel Sherman. In the liner notes for the album he wanted everyone to know how impressed he was by the way I handled "adult material," delivering an "adult repertoire that left both the press and the public gassed and flabbergasted. . . ."

I was a little flabbergasted myself by this time. "Ruby Baby," a song I'd heard for the first time at age fourteen in Tally's Poolhall, stuck out from the rest of that album like, well, a ruby in the rough. Everything else sounded like it was done by a whole other artist, one not nearly so confident or at ease with his material. In fact, after I recorded the song in Italian for the fans in the old country, I wasn't sure it was my material. I had a big following in Italy, so the idea of translating my hits into Italian was a natural. Columbia hired an Italian lyric writer and my grandfather helped me pronounce the words phonetically for the session. It all went smoothly, or so I thought, and "Ruby Baby" went on to top the Italian charts. It wasn't long after, when I went overseas on a promotional tour, that I met up with a local promoter in Rome. "'Ruby Baby'; it's a wonderful song," he said. "And the story, it's so interesting." The next thing I knew he launched into some tale all about a woman who couldn't pay her taxes and a lecherous collector who was after her. It took me a minute to realize that the lyric writer had taken more than a few liberties with the original tune!

Another cut on that first Columbia album was a thing called "The Loneliest Man In The World." The title should tell you something. If I couldn't knock Sinatra off his throne, maybe I could give Mario Lanza a run for his money. The funny thing about that record . . . we loaded so much operatics into those songs, sometimes they'd punch right out the other side and I'd end up reminding myself of Roy Orbison. One thing for sure, I didn't sound much like myself.

Sal, of course, was on the bandwagon, booking me into fewer colleges and more nightclubs, including regular stints at Jack Silverman's International right next door to the old Birdland, the Blue Room at the Roosevelt Hotel in New Orleans, and some other high-ticket supper clubs in Chicago, Boston, Philadelphia, and Miami.

When it came down to it, the role they were trying to cast for me was already more than adequately filled by Bobby Darin. Like he'd always done, Bobby was erasing the lines between "kid" and "adult" music time and again. He could take a standard and make it sound right in a juke box at the malt shop. At the same time, he was cutting rock 'n' roll that crossed over and back again. He was young, but he swung and had fun doing it.

We hung out a lot in those early days of '63, even though his health cut down on the carousing a little. After "The Wanderer" Bobby had taken to calling my music "Bronx blues," and when we were out together he'd still throw his arm around my shoulder and announce to everyone that the Bronx Bomber had arrived. But somehow, it didn't seem to fit anymore.

I was back to doing what came naturally; second guessing myself. Now, of course, it's easy to figure out why I had such a hard time sorting out my voice from all the others whispering in my ear. It was rooted back when I was a kid and was told over and over again that what I was feeling I shouldn't be feeling. That it was stupid or wrong or maybe just inconvenient. In a family like mine there were lots of strong feelings fogging up the air. But that's where they stayed, floating around us, because no one really knew how to express them. Or how to deal with them. When it came to picking the kind of music I wanted to do, the kind that would make me happy, all I knew was that if I stumbled on a really good song, it gave me a certain feeling, like a perfectly fitted pair of shoes. I had no idea how to go after that feeling, how to make it happen again. I couldn't trust my instincts, and when a singer loses that, all he's got is talent. Talent waiting to be exploited.

At first I figured that if this was the scene they wanted me to make, I'd do my best to oblige. I used to go down to the Copa, on my own or with Susan or Bobby, and check out all the big name acts booked there. One night it was the great Jimmy Durante and the highlight of the show was his "ha-cha-cha" version of "When You're Young at Heart." I really dug the way he did it: This guy was better than the Vic Damone clones they kept holding up to me. I mean, he just sat there on a stool with his hat in his hand and belted it out like he was going down for the last time. I had the bright idea of doing a record with Durante. Just the thing, I thought, to grab that "mature" audience. So I went home and wrote a song—a duet for the trouper and me. In the lyrics, an old guy gives a young kid the benefit of his years, spinning out homilies about love and life. It was kind of a retake of "Que Sera Sera" and I was sure I had a hit.

A couple of weeks later, Sal arranged for me to meet the Schnoz backstage after his show. Some publicist took me into the inner sanctum of his dressing room and introduced me as a very successful young songwriter and singer. If Durante had ever heard of Dion, he didn't let on. So I gave him my idea and sang a little of the tune for him. He didn't waste any time telling me exactly what he thought. "Son," he said, "you know I'm old. And I know I'm old. But *they* don't know I'm old. And I'd like to keep it that way. Why do you think I'm out there singing 'fairy tales can come true, they can happen to you, if you're young at heart?' Let's not pop their bubble, eh, kid?" I'd learned another valuable lesson—in this business you weren't allowed to get older, gracefully or otherwise.

Shortly after the ink had dried on my Columbia contract Susan and I honeymooned in Acapulco. Those first few months together really were like they always said it would be. Being man and wife was something so new and novel, it was almost as if we were acting out the parts, playing house and picking up our cues from all the movies we'd seen and magazines we'd read. The fact that we'd known each other for going on eight years didn't make much difference when it came to this strange new set-up. The truth was, neither one of us had any idea how to love, honor, and obey one another. They were just words, waiting to be tested.

Mexico was great, but even as a newlywed I had to keep the juggling act going. Laurie had released "Sandy" from my last album for them, so Columbia was anxious to rush out with a follow-up to "Ruby Baby." They picked a Carole King thing called "This Little Girl," and when I wasn't soaking up sun on the beach with Susan, I was back in the hotel room on the horn, working with Mersey to get a good mix for the song. He'd play me a version over the phone and I'd try to make it out through the long-distance static. Things were different back then.

They'd assign a guy like Mersey and he'd sort of oversee your record; but when it came down to the hands-on producing, that was left pretty much up to me. I was the artist, but I was also telling the musicians what to play, the singers what to sing, and generally building the whole sound from the ground up. Later, of course, you'd pay a lot of guys a lot of money to come in and turn the knobs, but for me, recording was like on-the-job training for a jack-of-all-trades. No matter what was going on, I could never get too far away from my career. They wouldn't let me. I wouldn't let myself.

Our first home as Mr. and Mrs. DiMucci was a deluxe apartment on Fifty-seventh street. We heard about the place from Cynthia and Barry Mann who lived one floor below us. The Manns had a friend, a young singer and songwriter named Neil Diamond, who used to drop by their apartment on a regular basis. I also got friendly with Neil, and on more than one Saturday afternoon we'd grab our guitars, head out to Central Park, and swap songs.

But Susan and I hardly had a chance to get used to our new home and life-style before duty called. The long-awaited European tour was about to get underway. I had barely enough time to squeeze in a couple of appearances on "Bandstand" and a quick cameo in another movie— this one called *Teenage Millionaire* with Jimmy Clanton. If you don't count *Ten Girls Ago*—and I suggest you don't—the Clanton quickie was actually the second movie I'd appeared in. I'd also done a couple of numbers in a Chubby Checker dance-fest called *Twist Around the Clock*. Neither of them were going to land me an Oscar, but my face was out there and that, as always, was all that mattered.

And it was all paying off like some kind of Hialeah exacta by mid-'63. I'd been voted most popular entertainer of the year by every trade magazine that mattered, had fan club chapters around the world, and guys on the payroll whose only job was to say no to incoming offers. But, even though I didn't notice it happening, something basic had changed. I wasn't alone anymore. Susan was by my side, watching everything with those big green eyes.

Once you get a handle on your hormones, once you get used to a new ring on your finger and a permanent addition in your bed, once all the novelty has worn off, marriage can seem like a contract full of fine print—one that you signed in the dark. Of all the things you don't count on—nylons in the shower and bills for stuff you didn't buy—I guess the hardest to get used to is the scrutiny. For going on six years I'd been flying high, fast and hard, without ever looking down. Everything was seasoned to my taste, suited to my temperament, set up to my specifications. It wasn't that Susan was trying to change all that; at least not at first. She was just there, taking it all in. The idea of having an innocent by-stander along on my joy ride was something I hadn't bargained for.

For one thing, it was hard to dazzle Susan with my newly acquired sophistication. She knew me too well, back when I was just a kid with greasy hair and zits. It's hard to snow someone who's seen you in the grip of raging adolescence and the very thing that for so long had made me feel comfortable around her—that familiarity —was suddenly getting on my nerves. I'd walk into a room and everyone else might be blinded by the brilliance of my famous dimpled smile. But Susan knew better. She could see through the act, past the airbrushed pretty boy and into a part of me, hidden and hurting, that I was trying so hard to deny. She was like a reminder of a time and place that had once seemed so hopeful, so full of promise. And no matter how much tap dancing I did, I could never blot that out.

If I'd been able to—if I could have remade myself in her eyes as the glamourous golden boy that everyone else saw—I don't know if we'd have even made it past the honeymoon. The truth is, I'm not sure she even *liked* the superstar who was trying so hard to sweep her off her feet. The guy she loved was simple, more genuine, nurtured in the neighborhood, part of a family. I'd lost touch with that guy and all Susan could do was hang on. And wait.

As my wife she had the nerve to say things to me, about me, that she'd held back on as my girlfriend. She shook me, rattled my confidence, and just at a time when I should have been soaring the highest. The European tour was first class all the way. The red carpet treatment you can get in London, Paris, Rome is something you'll never forget. My records had sold consistently just about everywhere on the continent and everywhere was where we went. Sitting in a room full of flowers and champagne with a view out my window of sunset over the Eiffel Tower was like a heady new high for me, proof of my world-class status.

And all the time Susan kept watching. She'd be there, running the gauntlet of flashbulbs and fans, standing backstage, or sitting ringside at the fanciest clubs. And she'd be there in the hotel room with me while I basked in the glow of my fame. And then one night, out of the blue, she asked me, "Dion, is this all you want? I mean, is this it?"

It was like being caught in a lie. Even though I didn't know what to say, I knew just what she meant. The capitals of Europe with the whole command performance bit . . . it might as well have been Montevideo in December.

I was spinning my wheels, trying to get a grip on something that would last. But it wasn't like I had that kind of control on my life anymore. Forces were in motion, payrolls had to be met, and records had to sell. I needed to slow down, for Susan, to give her my undivided attention as we settled into our marriage. But I didn't know how to give that, just like I didn't know how to slow down. Instead, I tried to catch her up into the crazed whirlwind I lived in.

When I got back to New York the first thing I found out was that the image molders had been real busy while the cat was away. Sal had hired Noel Sherman to write a brand-new nightclub act for me. To the tune of $15,000. I started rehearsals on the thing immediately and it wasn't too long after that I caught on to just how far into the mainstream they were pushing me. Sherman's whole show—the patter, the staging, the material—was a supper club extravaganza like the world had never seen.

Weeks passed while I went over and over the show. For the opening number I'd introduce myself as "The Last of the First-Name Singers" while in the background the choir crooned "D-I-O-N." The costume tuxes alone ran into thousands. With full frill at the cuff and the best satin sheen, I was ready for my big debut as a "serious" singer.

I guess I must have lost my cool, trying so hard to be

someone else. I'd put up with it for a long time, even climbed into the package for them. Finally, like a spring, I just bounced back. Maybe it was what Susan had been saying, about wanting more. Maybe it was just me catching up with myself. Whatever it was, I did it. And I'm glad.

One night, after a long rehearsal, I took everything home with me; all the arrangements for twenty-five-piece orchestra, augmented with violin and harps, all the scripts, the charts, the costumes, everything. I put it all together and, standing in the hallway of our apartment, at three in the morning, I threw it into the incinerator, sending $25,000 worth of show business schmaltz floating out across the Manhattan skyline. I'd finally found a way to blow money that really was satisfying.

CHAPTER 12

The Village

WHEN I kissed off the Last of the First-Name Singers, it was like grabbing on to a piece of my life again. I had my music back and I held on for dear life. I wasn't wet behind the ears anymore and whatever else my career was, it was also a job. I may be slow, but I was catching on—I knew as much about doing that job as anyone else. Sure, I wanted hits, but suddenly it was just as important to have them my way. I made a decision to be true to rock 'n' roll. Why not? I'd tried everything else.

Somewhere there's an arc that traces the rise and fall of every star. And somewhere near the top of that arc, where the air is thin and the view breathtaking, is where you finally realize that you've proved it, you've arrived. What you've done can't be undone. When that happens, when you reach that apex, you breathe a long sigh of relief. You're home free. Sure, you may have hits and flops from there on out, but, now and forever, they'll write that you were one of the best—the real thing with the right stuff. And maybe for the first time since you started getting paid to sing, you've got a real choice: You can keep gilding the lily or you can take your own shot. Either way, it's not gonna matter to your place in history. You're part of an exclusive club, with a lifetime membership. Now the only one you've got to please is yourself.

I'd had a taste of freedom and I was trying to go all the way with it. "I'm firmly convinced that singers, and critics, find fault with rock-and-roll because they can't understand it," I wrote on the liner notes to my new album *Donna the Prima Donna,* with a title tune that became my next Top Ten hit in the fall of '63. "Rock-and-roll" is an expression of the times—perhaps the strongest musical folk idiom of the Fifties and Sixties." It felt good, letting my fans know how *I* felt for a change, instead of how some composite of a hundred marketing schemes was supposed to feel.

And how I was feeling had a lot to do with what I was listening to. Columbia was really buzzing around that time, what with signing a young soul sister named Aretha Franklin in '61 and a high-intensity folksinger who called himself Bob Dylan, a year later. I took to hanging out up in the company's downtown offices, talking with the secretaries and making long-distance phone calls on Bob Mersey's line. It was exciting, walking up and down those hallways hung with gold records. It seemed like out of every room some kind of new sound was leaking.

And the most interesting noises were coming from John Hammond's crowded cubicle. Hammond was the legendary A&R man who had signed Dylan and would later pick up a Jersey kid for the label called Bruce Springsteen. He was a whole other kind of record company man, with a pure love for music that came through in his relationships with the artists. John gave you the feeling that what he was after was your best stuff, whether or not anyone else thought it had hit potential. And he had his own ways of bringing out that best, by sparking your creativity instead of stroking your ego.

His office was like a musical kitchen, where all kinds of exotic ear food was being brewed. Some days you'd be drawn down the hall by the sound of Aretha, pounding out a gospel tune fresh from her father's church on Hammond's piano. Or there'd be some earnest folkie, with a battered guitar and a mouth harp trying to pick up on what Dylan was laying down. Rock groups, folk quartets, classical scat—he just couldn't get enough of the real stuff and he never seemed to care where it came from. A well-crafted pop song put a smile on that lean, weathered face as quick as some vintage Chicago blues.

One day I heard a high, lonesome sound vibrating down the corridor like a train tearing through the night. I had to know what that was and John introduced me to the music of the great Lightnin' Hopkins. After that I just kind of set up shop on Hammond's sofa, soaking up the vintage music he'd so lovingly collected—Howlin' Wolf, Muddy Waters, and so many others, including the great Robert Johnson. Hammond told all kinds of tales—some legend, some gospel truth—about the great bluesmen. About how Robert Johnson had supposedly sold his soul to the devil to play his hypnotic licks and how his one and only album had sold 250,000 copies by word of mouth. No ad campaign, no flacks, no guest shots on Murray the K's show. Just one person telling another until there was a whole underground of true blues aficionados, passing the good word down the grapevine.

It was a club I wanted to be a part of. When I started to realize that all this amazing, expressive music had been around for a long time, I guess I felt a little resentful. How come nobody ever told me about this stuff? It was as if I'd finally found the well where the great artists came to dip for inspiration. One man and his guitar, telling it like it is . . . it was like a magnet, pulling me out of my tux and into a whole new world.

One of the artists Hammond especially liked was the blind blues preacher the Reverend Gary Davis, and when he told me that the old man was still alive and well and living in the Bronx, I flipped. Next day I made a pilgrimage to Davis's house, not all that far from the neighborhood, just to meet him and sit at his feet. His music was so simple, straight from his mouth to God's ears. It was raw, earthy, and rough cut and I'd never heard anything quite as powerful. Or moving. I had always thought my music, the songs we sang on the street corner, had come from other street corners in other neighborhoods across the city; just more local boys from Brooklyn or Harlem or the Lower East Side, putting it together, like we did, right out of the air. Now, spread out in front of me was a whole history lesson, tracing those rhythms and harmonies clear back to the rural crossroads of the deep South and beyond into the slave ships and over to Africa.

Davis was a kind, gentle man with a light that shone round him like a battered halo. He'd throw back his head and stare with those blind eyes into heaven, moaning and stuttering his 4/4 spirituals, stopping every once in a while to teach me a chord change or some snippet of lyrics. He was indulging me, a rich white kid anxious to feel the blues and, by the end of the day, I think some of it really soaked through from him to me. At least I felt pretty good as I stopped on the way home to buy a set of fingerpicks.

Dylan was another big influence on me. I'd met him once before, back at the Winter Dance Party when Bobby Vee had turned up to fill in for Buddy the night after the crash. Vee's keyboard player was a young kid named Zimmerman from Hibbing, just across the state line in Minnesota.

He'd come a long way since then. I'm not saying anything a hundred critics haven't said a thousand times better, but when Dylan burst on the scene, starting with his first Columbia album in '62, it marked the clear end of one era in American music and the quick beginning of a brand-new one. Before Bob, no one dreamed you could tie the simplest melodies, the roughest arrangements, and the quickest takes together and come up with music that made everything else sound half baked. It was readily accepted at the time that the kid had no voice, but, of course, that only enhanced his mystery and appeal. It wasn't how Dylan sang, or who was backing him up; it was what he said—his words—that stopped us all in our tracks. I fancied myself a songwriter because I could carve out a tune that caught people's ears. With Dylan, for the first time, I knew how much more music could do. He was funny and tormented, vulnerable and guarded, mysterious and up-front, all at the same time. I wanted to be like him because he was being himself.

Eventually I got tight with Dylan's producer at Columbia, a talented young guy named Tom Wilson. Wilson played some of the tracks Bob had been putting down in the studio and, as usual, it was awesome. Maybe I'd had my ear on the top of the charts too long, but it

suddenly occurred to me that, with some players jam-
ming behind some of those songs, he had a chance on
Top Forty radio. Wilson thought it was worth a try, so he
rounded up a bunch of session cats and took the tapes
down to the old Columbia studios. For the next couple of
hours Tom and I worked out some rock 'n' roll arrangements for Dylan's folk stuff and let the musicians rip. I
was right. It was totally in the pocket. Tom agreed and
took the doctored songs back to Dylan. He went electric
on his next album, *Bringing It All Back Home*. I really
liked that album. Later, when I'd drop in to listen while
he put his words into the razor-sharp work-outs cooked
up by players like Al Kooper and Mike Bloomfield, I realized this guy had rock 'n' roll in his blood from the very
beginning. It was all raw expression: Those sessions
cooked.

But that was only after he'd turned his back on the
folk scene, and in late '63, folk music was what was happening. And where it was happening was Greenwich Village, in clubs like Gerde's Folk City, the Bitter End, the
Gaslight, and a dozen other badly lit haunts with sawdust
on the floors and Chianti bottle candle holders sitting on
checked tablecloths. It was another big surprise—all the
while I'd been belting the Bronx blues, a scene had been
mushrooming under my nose, with music that was a lot
closer to the simple storytelling I'd learned from Hank
Williams than most of the Broadway melodies that I'd
been forced to croon. But once I discovered what was
happening down there around Washington Square, with
all the beatniks, conga players and girls in dark tights
and turtlenecks, I started hanging around in the Village.
There were great young songwriters everywhere, like
Kenny Rankin and John Sebastian. Richie Pryor was

part of it all, a fast-rising comic with a scorching routine. Every once in a while, some legendary blues cat would roll into town, Mississippi John Hurt or Sonny Terry and Brownie McGhee.

John, Kenny, Richie, and I hung together for a few months during those vintage Village days. Sebastian, with his huge smile and horn rims, had big plans for an electric jug band while Rankin just had a habit of being around great music. Pryor . . . well, Richard's comedy was kind of like rock 'n' roll, I always thought. It had the same dangerous edge, like cranking up a Fender. Anything could happen. We'd sit ringside at Steve Paul's Scene taking turns playing in a spontaneous set. Pryor had a hilarious running commentary on the scene and everyone really seemed to dig the rock and blues stuff I was doing. It was a mutual admiration society and sometimes we took our act on the road. Like the time Kenny Rankin drove nonstop, New York to L.A., in my T-Bird, singing all the way, with the help of some little white pills.

The music, especially the old stuff I'd started collecting, was opening me up to all sorts of new ideas, but, to be honest, half the stuff I was hearing from the folk elite left me a little cold. I always got the feeling that guys like Tom Paxton and Phil Ochs—two singer/songwriters touted as the best back then—were really just reporters, putting the news to music. It was like they'd collected headlines out of the *New York Times* and made up songs about all the trouble and strife that was beginning to bubble to the surface in the Sixties. For me, the personal connection was missing. But it wasn't even the music so much that gave me the feeling I'd found my niche. It was the glorious sense of possibilities. Yeah, being a musician really *was* all about expressing yourself, not trying to please people who'd never know the real you anyway. I guess there was more than a little ego wrapped up in thinking you could entertain by just letting it all hang out, but after so many years of playing the game, it was exhilarating to find out you could actually change the rules.

And rules *were* changing, all over the place. When Susan and I were in England with "Ruby Baby," I heard rumors about these four guys from Liverpool with funny haircuts. Haircuts! Being from the neighborhood, that caught my interest and so did their music. "Yeah, yeah, yeah," I remember thinking. "I get it." They reminded me of the Everlys but with something different . . . that edge again.

And naturally, I wanted to put the edge back into my sound. On *Donna the Prima Donna* I did. I'd caught hold of a whole lot of good music and it was bringing out the best in me, calling up the charge I got from that glorious Crotona Avenue noise, but without having to disguise it or water it down. I wrote "Donna the Prima Donna" to tease my sister and, like most of the record, it's full-on pop doo-wop in the best tradition of "Sue." Ditto "Can't We Be Sweethearts," a little stroll titled "This Little Girl of Mine," and, like a sweet refrain of a long gone past, a tune called "Oh Happy Day." I put in Richie Valens's "Donna," something I'd wanted to do for too long.

The real joy for me was in the hard-driving guitars and bottom heavy bass hitched onto songs like "Sweet, Sweet Baby" and a swift ditty I wrote called "Flim Flam." I covered straight blues, pounded out on a guitar and old upright piano with "Troubled Mind," and hit a jivey R&B stride on "This Little Girl," a tune that perfected my put-em-down songwriting style. No question about it, this was miles away from "The Loneliest Man in the World."

"Arranged and Conceived by Dion DiMucci" read the credits for *Donna the Prima Donna*. Mersey also took an arranging credit, which kind of points up some of the tensions developing between me and the label about this time. The Last of the First-Name Singers wasn't quite ready to grow up. Mersey had less and less to do with what was between the grooves, even though the label kept him in there to make sure things didn't get too out of hand.

At the same time, who could argue with success? In my own eyes I had gone from being a "performer" to being an "artist," but I still knew how to crank up a hit. "Donna" peaked in September of '63 and two months later I was back on top with "Drip Drop," a booming blues workout with a bruising guitar line from the Lieber and Stoller file. Like clockwork the tune climbed into the Top Ten.

It was right about then, from about as high as you could get, that I made the mistake of looking down for the first time.

CHAPTER 13

The River

IT was a long way to fall, and when I started to lose my balance, nothing could keep me on the tightrope. My world was turning inside out. Everything I'd ever done turned to choke me and everything I'd ever tried to hide from rose up to eat me alive. Day became night and I lived in the darkness, tumbling head over heels into the grip of the fears I'd been running from for all those years. You could say my luck had run out, but I'd never believed in luck. Luck was for suckers. You could say I finally caught up with myself, but I hadn't ever *found* myself. I'd become the sum of everyone else's dreams and fantasies, the ultimate disappearing act. I was Frances and Pasquale's kid, dressed in uptown threads. I was the man below the bottom line, a singing meal ticket. I was a husband, a son, a man with no future. I was a junkie.

Nowadays you hear a lot about just saying no, about what drugs can do to your body and brain. But it's really the spirit they poison, eating away at your conscience like acid. The day I'd snorted that first white line and walked like a king through the tenement streets was the day I cut myself off from ever facing what was wrong with me, Dion, the man behind all those masks. I was thirteen years old and that's where I stayed. I just stopped growing, stuck there on the trembling edge of manhood. It was smack that sucked me into thinking only about myself, got me addicted to blaming others for my problems, or simply turned me away, to pretend they didn't exist. Getting into heroin, a need with my name on it, was also nobody's idea but mine. I wasn't just some clean slate that anyone could scrawl a message on—my parents, my handlers, my fans. I had a choice. I may have been looking for a way out of my past, but what drugs killed wasn't just the bad memories. Hope and joy and childlike faith withered and died, too. I was responsible for all the ways I'd reacted to what was going down around me, even when I couldn't do anything about it. The shame I felt at the laughter of my uncles, the fear behind my mother's brave tears, the anger at my dad's tattered dreams of glory. I owned it all.

Smack made my dreams seem real, so real that, after a while, there was nothing better. From that very first snort of the pure stuff, the junkie inside me came alive. I didn't stand a chance of ever seeing the truth or putting things in perspective or living a useful life in service to anybody but myself. Sure, I'd quieted all those voices inside that made me feel so guilty, but I'd also gagged the one that made me feel bad about who I'd become. If it hadn't been for the chemicals that seeped into my soul, I think I might have even found love from my parents, despite their own problems, their own addictions. I wasn't a righteous guy messed up by a bad home life. I was a drug addict. That was my problem and it was brought on by self-centeredness. When was the first time I realized I couldn't change circumstances or conditions to suit myself? That day my dad threw me off the raft? Back when they shipped me off to New Jersey? Or let me hang in the sewer to prove my manhood? Whenever it was, that's when the need to get high, to fix reality, swept over me in a wave.

I could have just stayed away from the things that were causing me hurt and pain. But there was no place remote enough to escape myself. I could have faced them down, but that takes courage and I still hadn't learned how to pray for that.

Or I could have tried to numb the ache, which is what I chose. For a while it even worked; long enough, anyway, that when I finally got hip it was too late. I was hooked, as sure as the meanest addict, sweating and moaning on a filthy mattress somewhere. Only I was living like a king. As a kid playing stickball on the street, I might even have laughed to see a guy like me tooling down Crotona Avenue, someone so puffed up with himself, but so sick inside. I might have let the air out of his tires or knocked his hat off his head and run away, laughing.

But I wasn't laughing now. I was hurting. Bad. And moving so fast I could hardly hold a breath of air in my lungs. "Slow down, D!" Ricky always used to say in the old days. "Watch the guys who pitch pennies. The guy who looks like he isn't trying so hard always lands them right. The harder you try, the harder it is to do. Relax, buddy." But I couldn't stop to talk to him. I had planes to catch and scenes to make. I was running all the time, toward something or away from something and finally I just got tired. Enough was enough. Once the engines cut out, all you can do is try and hang on for the sickening slide down. And there's no guarantees you're gonna make it. Like I said, it's a long way to fall.

By 1964 I was using every day, mainlining smack and dabbling in amphetamines, doing lots of grass, lots of wine. When I wasn't down in the Village acting like an artist, or up at the label acting like a star, or at home acting like a husband, I was in an underground parking lot acting like a junkie. My best connection was the guy who parked cars at my plush East Side apartment building and when he would go uptown to score, I'd take his place. There I was, Mr. Sensational, jockeying cars for hours on end, waiting for my man. We'd tie-off together, huddled over the electric heater in the change booth, and afterward I'd wander off into the night, like a dead man.

Later, nodding out on the sofa, with a guitar in my hand or out at some club with a cigarette burning down between my fingers, I'd swim up through the haze and look around. Sure thing, I thought, I had life whipped. Music itself had become like a drug, a narcotic that numbed all those endless hours I had to kill, basking in my glory. Only it wasn't working anymore. As '63 slid into '64, and the year unwound like blacktop through the fog, I did less and less serious recording. It was like all the freedom had turned sour and the ability to do things my way only put me in a new kind of prison. I was playing to please myself, all right, because most of the time I was the only one who heard my music. I'd swallow a handful of uppers and play the guitar for thirteen straight hours before falling into a thick, dreamless sleep that left me drained, with no memory of all the great chord changes I'd uncovered. I told myself I was getting back to my roots, but all I was really doing was digging myself deeper into a self-indulgent rut. I was writing, sure, but after the applause starts to get tinny and the glare of the lights gets to your eyes, what's the point of aiming for one more hit? Who needs it?

You'd think the bitterest blow would've been the overdue realization that fame was a trick, done with smoke and mirrors. Money, adoration, headlines, and your name in lights—I had it all, and all it meant was that more of the same was never enough. But there's worse things than waking up sadder and wiser. Like not waking up at all.

As suddenly as they'd come, the hits dried up. Musical tastes were changing and I probably could have kept up, but I'd stopped caring. There was a junkie's genie who watched over me and his advice was, "everything's cool." I was starting to drift further and further out on a tide of drugs, blunting the edge that had kept me on top. It happens to the most careful addict—after a while you start to nod and mumble and forget what it was you ever wanted in the first place. I started recording all sorts of esoteric blues and actually released two more singles: Willie Dixon's "Hoochie Coochie Man" and another old standard, "Chicago Blues." But by that time it was all coming apart. Those tunes were stark, scary renderings, with about as much mass appeal as the originals. Mersey was gamely trying to make some sense of my rambling and Wilson actually liked the feel I was getting, but no one was kidding themselves anymore. In the midst of recording a new album, a straight blues and folk collection called *Wonder Where I'm Bound* Mersey started walking out on the sessions, frustrated and disgusted. I barely noticed.

What I was noticing was Columbia's lack of interest in releasing any new material. Aside from those two blues tunes and the album—which included some Dylan, some Woody Guthrie, and more Willie Dixon—I was conspicuous only for my absence on the charts. Columbia was riding it out, waiting and hoping that I'd get back on track.

I was going into the third year of my five-year stint with Columbia when I walked in and told them I wanted out, that I couldn't record for them anymore. I needed time to get into my guitar, I said, telling myself that I wanted to develop my songwriting without the pressure to produce hits. All I really wanted was to be left alone.

I wasn't worried about money. Even with my parents still on the payroll I had more than I knew what to do with. I could've holed up indefinitely.

Columbia wouldn't release me. I was locked into a cycle of singles, albums, promotions, and concerts that had taken on a life of its own. And taken over mine. I put a band together, a hot bunch of players from the Bronx, and Sal booked an East Coast tour. Meanwhile, I had found a new Dr. Feelgood, my next-door neighbor, whose stash was never more than a door knock away. My intake doubled and, when you're in that condition, it's best not to stray too far from your supply base.

But I had these gigs, including this big supper club in Boston, run by some guys with broken noses and shiny suits. We were scheduled to play a long weekend, but by Friday night I'd run out of junk. There was only one thing to do. I jumped into my car and tore back to New York, fighting the sweats until I could find my connection. Only he wasn't home. The next half-dozen frantic hours I spent on the street looking for a bundle—twenty-five bags. I finally scored and raced back to Boston, but it was too late—I'd missed the Saturday show.

Sunday went off like a dream—big house, big encores, the whole bit—until I went backstage to settle up. Someone closed the door behind me and I turned around to see three guys with baseball bats. They were quite serious about breaking my legs for missing the show. We don't do business that way, the club owner wanted me to know. We honor our commitments. He wasn't kidding, but in the end they let me go. "Out of respect for your lovely wife, Susan," was what they told me as I slinked away in a cold sweat.

Blowing dates was just another symptom of my sickness. One of the reasons those Boston boys went off on me, I think, was what had happened in Providence a couple days before, when I grabbed a promoter by the throat and shoved him against the wall for some petty infraction. It was like I was back at the Institute for Living or maybe even in the Baldies again. Only now I was pushing the wrong people around. The word was getting out . . . Dion was trouble. Stay away.

And everyone was doing their best to oblige. Even Susan, who had walked into this marriage with her eyes open, could only stand back and watch as the flames started to lick at me. She was patient, loving, and concerned but I don't think she realized the extent that smack had taken hold of me and even if she had, she was too young, too inexperienced, to handle it. The question she asked me back in Europe—"Is this it?"—had never been answered, so she just let it lie. She didn't want to admit to herself what was happening to me, much less confront the monster I'd become. There was nothing left to do but back off, trying to keep out of harm's way as the demons nipped at my heels. We never argued much. It was as if we both knew how helpless we were and how afraid that, by opening one door, we'd have to open another. In a way, I think Susan was kind of a habit for me, too. I guess when you're a junkie, everything gets obsessive. My wife, who worked so hard to learn to accept, was accepting too much. I was walking through our marriage like a zombie. And she was following because there was no place else to go.

The months rose and fell with deadening regularity, spring into summer, summer into fall, fall into a bleak, unforgiving winter. And with each passing day I sank further into myself, like a man with a strange disease that eats away at him from the inside, leaving only a brittle shell. Maybe it all seems kind of sudden—one minute on top of the world, the next with one foot in the grave—but this was the third act payoff to a play that had been running for almost thirty years. I'd cycled in and out of heavy heroin use since I was a teenager, each year surrendering a little more of my will and self-esteem, each year finding reality a little harder to face. Then, one day, there just wasn't any more reality. I'd finally obliterated what I couldn't control, and with it, any claim to being aware, active, or even alive. All that was left was the naked need, like a beggar at the door.

That East Coast tour was like a last gasp. I'd been ripping up the road at a hundred miles an hour and now, nothing. Fans kept writing, agents kept calling, but the whole machine was grinding to a halt. It was a relief in a way, like pulling the plug on a terminal patient, even though at the time I had no idea that it was the beginning of the end. After all, I'd been to the peak. I didn't have to come down until I was good and ready. What I didn't realize was that while I was up there admiring the view, the parade had passed me by. There was a whole new kind of music getting over now, a whole new kind of cool. The Fifties were finished and, in a business where you're not allowed to get old, the rules say adapt or die. I couldn't bend, so I was beginning to break.

I honestly believed that I shouldn't say a word about what was going on inside me. Not to Susan, not to anyone. It would be a sign of weakness, proof that I'd been wrong about everything. If I copped to the frustration, the terror, the isolation, I'd have to cop to my powerlessness and the simple fact that I couldn't cut it anymore. If that happened, I'd lose respect. I might start getting treated like my father, like something less than a man. I'd have to face my own weakness, the helpless feeling that came with defeat. I'd have to ask for help. I would rather have died. It was one of the few choices left to me.

By 1965, I knew something had to change and soon. And the only thing I could think to do was fix the exterior. New York was a rat race, I decided. The city was dirty, crowded, and smelled bad. What you need, I told myself, is a change of scenery. We hunted around and found this spectacular A-frame nestled in the mountainous woods in Nyack, overlooking the span of the Tappan Zee Bridge and the long, lazy flow of the Hudson.

The house was like a Swiss chateau, with a solid glass front and fireplaces on all three stories. It was the biggest and best birdcage yet and a great place for weekend parties. I'd invite up all the musicians I knew from the Village along with the local painters, sculptors, and writers and, more often than not, they'd bring along the hip new drugs—LSD, mescaline, magic mushrooms.

Giving me acid was like giving an epileptic a loaded gun. It wasn't like smack, or pot, or any other pill I'd ever taken to make me happy. It only made reality seem more real, taking all the blackness inside and magnifying it into a perfect blackness, a pitch darkness with no light at the end of the tunnel. Acid made me realize that nothing made sense, that it never had. It was an overwhelming terror that sunk its teeth into my mind. I couldn't break free from the despair.

Finally, inevitably, the day came when all the party-goers were gone and, by some terrible accident, I found myself completely alone. I didn't know where Susan was; I might as well have been the last man on earth, standing on the terrace, looking out across the river, high on acid with a bottle of scotch in my hand. With each belt I knocked back, I became more convinced that there was nothing left for me and no way out but the grave. I decided to commit suicide, but almost as soon as the certainty rose up with a rush of nausea, I started cursing myself—not fate, my father, or fickle fame—for being a coward and a fool. Stumbling back into the house, I stood in front of the mirror. "You creep," I sobbed. "You pathetic creep." What happened to that kid who once enjoyed life to the fullest, who loved music and people and walked through the neighborhood streets with a bounce to his step, his head held high, excited, free? Where was he, I asked, but I knew the answer. He was standing in front of me, drunk and stoned and helpless. It was then that I heard my own voice. It said, "God help me."

Sodden with rage and misery, I walked out of the house, settled on killing myself by driving my car over the bridge. But the car was gone. Somebody had borrowed it. Stolen it, maybe. I had no idea what had happened, no memory of handing over the keys. I stood there staring at the empty parking space. I couldn't go back into the house. I couldn't drive off the bridge. So I started walking, down Route 9W toward town. The sun had set. Night was coming on.

Somewhere inside of me, though, a light broke—the answer to my three-word prayer. Sanity fell like blessed rain and I felt something like the presence of God—a quiet, calm, loving grace that stopped me in my tracks. "I never knew you were real," I whispered and listened as the breeze in the trees answered. "I've never talked to You. I don't know how. Tell me what should I do." For maybe the first time in my life, there was no need for explanations or excuses. Nothing I could say or do to fix things. No expectations. No disappointments. No fear.

What should I do? Accept, receive, let go, the Presence said. Let it happen. And like the smell of a flower, like the smile on a kid, like a day when clouds as big as sailing ships skip across the sky—like a miracle—that's what I did. I let go.

And when I did, the falling finally stopped. I landed, not crushed and broken, but safe in Someone's arms. I don't know how long I stood there, how many miles of river flowed out to the sea while God held me tight. I don't even remember the cop car pulling up, or the officer walking up to me. But I do know what I said when he asked me if everything was alright. I turned and smiled and nodded. "Everything is fine," I said, and when he wanted to know if he could give me a lift somewhere I just shook my head. "It's such a beautiful night. I think I'll walk for a while."

CHAPTER 14

Kicking

I WISH I could say that was that. End of story. Good-bye and amen. But things aren't that simple. At least not for me. We've all heard stories about moments in time when somebody does a 180-degree turn right into a new way of life. People call it conversion, the moment of truth, a peak experience, or a hundred other names that explain the unexplainable. I'm not saying those things don't come down. It's just that, for me, healing, real healing, was slow in coming. And when it did, it wasn't all at once, like some cosmic cure-all. It was one day at a time.

And the days of 1966 were the bleakest in my life, an unending succession of hours divided between remorse and rebellion. The warm glow of that night in Nyack would quickly fade, leaving all the dull aches behind. Nothing—no mystic moment under the stars, no voice in my head or pat on my back—was going to soothe away a lifetime of sincere self-destruction. God wasn't waving any magic wands. Sure, I'd bottomed out. So what? When you get enough rope, it's no big accomplishment to hang yourself. I was still shooting smack, still letting my marriage wither from neglect, still letting my career sink slowly into the setting sun. I knew I was sick. I just didn't know how to get better.

What I did know was that I'd run out of time. Staring into the blackness at the bottom of the river had proved that. I wanted to get right. At least I *wanted* to want to. And what I couldn't do for myself, Susan tried to do for me. Physically I was falling apart fast, prey to every flu and cold that swept in on the New York winter winds, my arms marred by needle marks and abscesses—the classic sniffling, underfed junkie. I was a daily user now and anyone who's lived with an addict, whatever his jones may be, knows the tension that can build up, waiting for the inevitable crash. Susan was playing that waiting game, patiently and compassionately, even when the stakes got dangerously high. Of all the things she was—a faithful friend, a devoted wife, a woman in love—she was also, sometimes, just a person, scared and alone and touched by the madness that had infected me.

I guess it finally got to be too much for her one drizzly day in the autumn of that nightmarish year when, for what must have seemed like the ten thousandth time, I was making my Manhattan rounds, looking for a fix. Susan was with me, dragged along for company, silently sitting through one street corner liaison after another. By now I was making no attempt to disguise my all-consuming love for junk—more seductive, more demanding than any woman, any hit record, could ever be. Silence was the rule between us, silence enforced by anger and fear. But keeping it quiet couldn't keep it hidden—not anymore.

After what must have been hours cruising through seedier and seedier neighborhoods, Susan finally started to crumble. All the years of not letting herself feel, of patching up the wounds, turning away the resentment, and glossing over the neglect finally found a voice. She began to cry, at first softly, then with an intensity I'd never seen in her before. I'm not even sure what I said: I might have played the concerned husband and asked her what was the matter; I might have let the junkie loose and told her to shut up. Whatever it was, it was one step over the line. She turned on me in a fury and started flailing with her fists, striking wherever she could, hoping it would hurt. I tried to duck her blows, actually surprised that my wife had finally snapped. But she wouldn't stop and that's when I started to get mad. I screeched to a halt and, through a hail of punches and tears, threw open her door and tossed her into the street. I roared off, leaving her alone in a strange part of town to find her own way home, to protect the baby that, only a few months before, had started to grow inside of her. If I even cared, I didn't know how to show it. I couldn't feel anything, not even the pain that came when, later that night, five guys jumped me in an alleyway after they'd seen me finally cop the junk my body was aching for.

Through the thick mist of my own delusions, Susan seemed like a shadow—a voice and a face that I recognized but couldn't place. I knew she was someone who had once meant everything to me, but who could now no longer fill the hole where those feelings had lived. There was something strange and only half real about this stranger who had tied herself to my life. I can't say I was grateful to have her around, that I ever thanked fate for her faithfulness. I took her totally for granted, like my own heart, pumping blood through the long night. I never thought about what she might need, or want, or wish for.

In this, and a hundred other ways, I was turning her into something less than human, less than a woman or a wife. I robbed her of her self-respect, her security, and her future and when she got pregnant, it was as if she were desperately laying claim to some part of that future, striking out against the desperation and loneliness. The child she nurtured was her way of letting life affirm itself again, like in the old days when we were young and the whole world hummed with anticipation. Maybe her husband was the worst kind of junkie, lost in his own self-ishness, but that didn't mean she had to give up on the gift God had bestowed on her—the ability to be a mother and love a baby. That I couldn't take away.

It would hurt me now too much to bear if I believed that my baby girl was an "accident," something that just happened while I was half-stepping across the littered stage of my life. It would hurt me to believe that, like any accident, she could just as easily not have ever happened. But what would hurt me worst of all was if my daughter believed that. Of all the hard things I've had to say in this book, one of the hardest is that I was too lost and too hurt and too weak to believe I could ever be a father. Susan made that choice for me and it was only later, on my knees, that I understood that there are no "accidents." No mistakes. However hard I tried to throw myself away, God was there, protecting, preserving, using the tools at hand to perfect His plan. What I couldn't do for myself, He did for me, holding it all in place—my family, my career, even my life—until, at long last, I could stand on my own two feet and begin to count my blessings.

And that wouldn't come easy. There was no reason why it should. You can't erase years of abuse like you would a dirty word on a blackboard and even when I finally realized that the walls were closing in on me, there was still no guarantee I was going to make it through. Nick-of-time escapes only happen in the movies, and for every story told by a reformed junkie, there's a hundred more you never hear because the guys who could tell you are dead. I didn't just wake up one day and discover, like a fat man at a feast, that I'd had enough. It was a slow awakening that maybe began that night, looking out over the river, realizing that nothing was working anymore. Least of all heroin.

There's a saturation point you reach when you pump enough poison into your veins, a moment when you finally understand that the stuff has seeped into your core, the deepest parts of who you are. In some terrible way it *becomes* who you are. Right then, you're faced with a choice: to keep going and embrace death or try and fight it. The scales are perfectly balanced; where you throw your weight will decide how you live out the rest of your days. It's no joke; you know, all of a sudden, that you can't kid yourself anymore, that you can't pretend you'll be quitting next week, next month, next year. Each time you fix makes the commitment more real. It's like staring into the mouth of a rabid dog; it's a fear so real you're scared to do anything but give in. Or start scrambling for the strength to get away.

I was doing some hard scrambling by the fall of '66. Smack, instead of getting me high, was starting to get me low. Instead of a warm rush tingling through my body, I was starting to feel a cold chill freezing my blood. This wasn't what I'd bargained for. The magic powder that turned the world into my oyster suddenly seemed like the oldest, meanest con in the book, a lie that didn't even bother to disguise itself anymore. I felt life draining out of me with every nickel bag. In its place, a numbness crept up my spine. I needed professional help.

Only problem was, the pros refused to take me on. I made the rounds of hospitals, looking for someone, some program, to build a bridge over the abyss, but no one in their right mind would accept a junkie in my advanced state of decay. Maybe it had something to do with my attitude. I thought I was doing them a favor—a famous singing star looking to lend a little prestige to their patient roster—like I'd be signing an exclusive contract or something. But they didn't see it that way. I'd stroll into the lobby as if to say "Here I am. Take me. I'm yours," and they'd just hustle me right back through the revolving doors. I got thrown out of some of the finest institutions in New York City.

When I finally talked Mount Sinai Hospital into admitting me, I was on the far side of desperate. Susan was right up front about pulling my strings; if impending fatherhood would push me into getting help, then she'd stick out her belly and waddle around for all it was worth. But I didn't need much convincing. Only answers. Which was the last thing I got, sitting in my pajamas in the psycho ward, watching the loonies and wondering what a nice guy like me was doing in a place like this. They'd scheduled daily sessions with a shrink and we'd spend hours just getting to know each other. He'd watch how I folded my hands or flicked my cigarette ashes, and I'd watch him watching me. After a while it got to where I was second guessing everything I did: Was my hair combed a little too neatly? Was I breathing too hard? Not hard enough? I'd try to figure out what he was thinking by the way he folded *his* hands and flicked *his* ashes, and round and round we'd go, day after day, getting nowhere except bored and frustrated.

Nights were a different story. The shakes, the sweats, the cramps and cravings were only symptoms of the sickness that was chewing me up. I was kicking junk, all right, and it was a slow, torturous process, but to tell you the truth, that was the easy part. I could endure the worst case of cold turkey. I had to. I knew that now. What wasn't so simple, what stayed stubbornly unendurable, was the thought of facing the cruel, cold world solo, without a crutch to carry me through.

Even after all this time, it hadn't sunk in: I was still trying to fix things, to get it all tucked away in neat little pigeon holes, to make it work the way I wanted, I needed, it to. The climb to the top made no more sense than the plunge to the bottom. I was helpless to control anything—my career, my family, myself—but still I tried, hopelessly pulling strings that had been cut and dangling from the time I was a kid, still trying to deal with all those hurts and resentments and disappointments that were bundled up like a fist in my gut. Sure, I could take the junk away from the junkie, but that didn't get me any less hooked. Smack wasn't my problem. It never was. It's just a chemical, no less evil than the use we put it to. And the use I'd put it to was to smother the deep sense of insecurity that had been my constant companion ever since I could remember. I wanted to do everything myself—to never have to depend on another person for a dime or the time of day. I thought self-confidence would take me all the way. I had the will to win. What else did I need?

There was only one catch. Along with the will to win

came the fear of failure. Along with having it all my way came the burden of holding it all together. Along with the need to fix everything came the loud crashing of a little world falling to pieces. My problem couldn't have been solved by a squad of shrinks in a maximum security detox ward. My problem was that I could never let go, and the harder I held on, the less I had to hold on to.

I was running in tighter and tighter circles, dogging my own tail, chased by my own shadow. When what it is and what you think it is become the same thing, your head starts playing nasty little tricks on you. I was convinced that I was the topic of everyone's whispered conversations, the focus of everyone's stolen glances. Some poor guy would be standing by the window, looking out onto the leafless trees of the exercise yard and, even with his back turned, I was positive he was checking me out with those eyes in the back of his head. I'm sure if I'd watched a football game on TV, I'd have been convinced that they were cracking jokes at my expense in the huddle. There was something about close-up exposure to mental illness that brought out my own craziness, feeding the paranoia during the long, listless days with nothing to do.

I had no way to get better, no way to make it work except my own stubborn will to survive. Inside of a couple of weeks I was clean, getting my health back, putting color in my cheeks and meat on my bones. But, while I might have felt like a new man, it was the same old Dion inside. Junk almost did me in, but there was a prospect even more frightening than the inevitable overdose I'd been heading for. And there was no way I could clean that up. It couldn't have been more than a couple of days between finally getting the snake out of my veins and the time I plunged headlong into booze, slipping the aides a couple of bucks for a fifth and drinking myself right back into the same cramped cell I'd just climbed out of. "Name your poison," they say, when you step up to the bar. "Anything'll do," was always my answer. Anything at all.

Drinking was an improvement, I told myself. It was legal. It was cheap. It was easy to come by. And, when it got right down to it, if I drank enough—if I really worked at putting myself away—it was as good as the purest China white. Anything really *would* do. Anything to drive away the demon that called himself by my name. After a month at Mount Sinai, I walked away, free from junk but still a slave to my need. Nothing had changed but the name of the game.

My daughter Tane was born in November. The name? In the hospital I'd been reading a book with a character called Tain, or at least I think that was the name. I've never really been sure if I'd just read it wrong, but it really didn't matter. It fit . . . she looked like a Tane. I picked her and Susan up to take them home on one of those pitiless winter mornings when the sky looks like the bottom of a skillet and the sleet sweeps across the frozen streets. As I drove down the Cross Bronx Expressway, through neighborhoods that even then were beginning to look like a war zone, I remember looking into her bassinet, watching this little angel fast asleep on the seat beside me, totally helpless, totally trusting. I felt dirty: as soiled and grimy and run down as the city all around me. I wanted to split, anywhere, as long as it was far away. Someplace where I could pretend that everything was going to be alright. For Tane, for Susan, and for me.

Maybe it's hard to understand how a man could

need to hide that much, how his reflection in a mirror could be his own worst enemy. There's lots of people who never had the kind of breaks I did, whose childhoods made mine look like a picnic, and whose prospects were somewhere between dim and grim. Somehow they made it, steering a course around all the poisons that ease the pain in this world of hurt, facing down the odds and finding the dignity they deserve. Why couldn't I pull myself up by my own bootstraps, dust myself off, and get serious about life? What gave me the right to throw it all away?

When it comes to suffering we all could write a book and stain every page with the tears of what might have been. There's nothing special about me, nothing that a few lines on a hit record chart couldn't sum up. I was a kid from the Bronx who'd had it all and lost it all and if you wanted to write something on my tombstone back in the waning days of '66, one word might have done the trick: "Why?" I'd spent my whole life looking for the answer to that question, without ever really knowing what I was after. I don't think it was the looking that was killing me. I think it was the not knowing.

CHAPTER 15

Jack

THEY say God works in mysterious ways, His wonders to reveal. Who am I to argue? He could have grabbed me by the collar and jerked me into reality any time He wanted. He could have short-circuited my selfishness and turned me into a saint on the spot, right there in the psycho ward or on the road to Nyack. Let's face it, He could have done anything He wanted. But what He chose to do was what worked the best. I guess that's why He's God and we're us.

There really was only one way to teach me how to respect myself again, to accept reality and find joy in my responsibilities. Leaving behind all the bad memories, finding a new life in another town, wasn't going to do the trick. Neither was the concern of my wife, my responsibility for my daughter, or the fear of becoming an also-ran on the musical merry-go-round. I don't even think parting the Red Sea would have impressed me at that point. That one-word question, "Why?" kept eating at me as 1967 came creeping round the corner. But even if the answer had been printed in banner headlines in the

New York Times, I don't think it would have made a difference. What I really needed was what I finally found: the flesh and blood proof of another human being—someone who'd been there and back, who could understand what had happened to me, not because he'd read about a case like mine, but because he'd *been* a case like mine. At that late date, the only thing that was going to sink in was something I could touch and feel and hold on to. For me, the mystery of God isn't found in flashy miracles and spiritual fireworks. It's in the way He uses simple, ordinary people and everyday situations to get the job done. I'd been outsmarting myself for too long. Like a little kid, I need to learn a lesson.

At least, that's the way my case was handled. Now, on the far side of those days, I can honestly say I'm glad He took me the long way round, even though at the time I would have given anything to beat the rap. I almost drove myself off a bridge—it was that close when God stepped in—but I still had to deal with the consequences of what I'd become and the trail of broken promises I'd left behind. That's the way it had to be. I can dig that now, even if it stung like salt in a wound back then.

If I'd just walked out of that hospital delivered from fear, and the habits that hid the fear, I might never have known how much was at stake—what I had to lose and what I had to gain. I would have missed the whole point, the real reason I never made my date with the river that night. I would have been just one more lucky stiff, saved by the skin of his teeth. But most important, I never would have had the privilege of seeing God work through a man named Jack.

Nineteen sixty-seven—the whole year—was like

one long lost weekend. I'd go for a couple of months without drinking before falling back into the bottle and making up for lost time. But it wasn't just the booze that made that year seem like somebody else's bad dream. I wasn't making music, hits or otherwise, and I couldn't work up enough interest to try. With nothing to do but sit home and collect royalty checks, drink and brood, I was fulfilling the show business stereotype—the over-the-hill superstar, burnt out at the ripe old age of twenty-eight.

Columbia finally read the handwriting on the wall and let my contract die a natural death—a sad end to the label's first rock 'n' roll signing. I'd still play live on occasion—blues stuff, mostly, along with the hits—but the thrill had definitely long gone. I started painting as an outlet for some of the anxiety and nervous energy that was burning a hole in my life. I'd take a handful of uppers, and, just like those pointless hours alone with my guitar, I'd turn out canvasses to please myself. Some part of me, I guess, was still convinced that creativity could give me the fulfillment I was desperate for. But being creative for me was just a habit now. The sense of accomplishment was dead. More important, so was the fun.

When I wasn't slinging a paintbrush, I was hanging out with friends—guys I'd known for a long time, from the neighborhood. Guys, I found out, who were a lot like me. Like Donny Moffet, who I'd hung with clear back to my days at Ermondo's. What I liked about Donny was what I liked about being back with the old crowd. He was simple, with no airs or big ideas—someone who'd been around the block a few times and learned something, the hard way. I kind of missed that in some of the circles I'd been traveling in.

What I'd never known about Donny was that he'd

been an alcoholic for years and, by the time we hooked up again, had only recently licked the bottle. I could see it in his eyes—he'd settled something with himself—and that interested me and scared me at the same time. He'd come over to the house and listen while I talked and drank. Once in a while he'd tell me about what he'd been through and, even though I didn't want to hear, some of it was making sense. Seeds were being planted. And what came through mostly was his acceptance. He never talked down, never criticized or lectured. He just shared. Donny knew it was a long road back.

Naturally, falling into the past put me in touch with the Belmonts again. Carlo, Freddie, and Angelo had been through their own strange sagas. From a distance of ten years, it all looked pretty funny. Spaghetti on our T-shirts and pounding out rhythms on the D Train were parts of a life so long ago it might as well have been a fairy tale. And in true fairy-tale tradition, we got the act together again. We even got a pretty good sized advance from ABC Records to do a reunion album, but I think we knew all the time that you can never go home again. Not really. We might have fooled the public, but we never could have fooled ourselves. Too much water . . . too many bridges.

And I was finally faced with just one too many slammed doors. I had to do something, make some kind of choice, take some sort of action. The months had come and gone with the tide, bringing booze and boredom and broken dreams in their wake. The phone wasn't ringing much and if it did I wouldn't have answered it. I wasn't a junkie anymore, but I might just as well have been main-lining scotch, the way I let booze take me over. This, I told myself, was a dead end. What I needed was a new life.

If you're born in New York, and you want to go to paradise, you head for Miami. Don't ask me why, but there's something about that spells the good life. The weather, sure, the beaches, and the babes—but it's more than that. To move to Florida is to get your little parcel of the American Dream. It's like a gold watch from God, the place you go after you've arrived.

Maybe there was some part of me that just wanted to retire, to be put out to pasture with nothing left to prove. Maybe there was a listless voice deep inside that kept telling me the race was run. Maybe my life felt like it was already over. To tell the truth, I didn't have a clue. All I knew was that Miami sounded good all of a sudden, the soothing solution to stagnation. I even sobered up in those last months of '67, conscious that I wanted to get my new, problem-free, life off to a clean start. "Wish me luck," I imagined myself saying to the city where I was born as I followed the moving van south, wife and kid by my side. But New York just squatted there, belching smoke. Some things never change.

And I guess I'm one of them. That truck may have been full of our furniture, but that wasn't all we were hauling down to Florida. All the things I was running away from also hitched a ride along the seaboard and made themselves right at home in Miami's warm ocean air, like visiting viruses from the slums. I was exactly the same guy, only wearing a Hawaiian shirt instead of a fox-collared overcoat. Welcome to paradise.

But it wasn't just more of the same that was waiting for me in that lush, green jail. There was someone there with the key to let me out. I'd come to die, but Jack Butterfield saved my life.

He was a big man, beefy and bald, and his face got real red when he laughed. He had a smile you could see from a mile away and a way of talking right to you with his eyes. He could have been someone's Dutch uncle, but he was my father-in-law. Jack Butterfield was in his mid-fifties when my family and I moved in with him until we could find a house of our own. He'd come to Florida from the Bronx like millions before and after him, only Jack wasn't interested in retiring. A respected maître d' at the Fontainebleau Hotel, he had turned his natural instincts for serving people into a solid, secure living for himself and Midge, Susan's mom. Jack also knew what life was like inside a bottle. For fourteen years before our paths crossed, he hadn't let liquor pass his lips. He'd beaten the one thing I never could beat—the need.

But it wasn't Jack's willpower that impressed me. It was his peace of mind. Those first two weeks at his house, I watched him closely, not because I wanted to get to know a man I'd never let into my life before, but because I'd never met anyone quite like Jack. In the morning he'd be very quiet, getting up before the rest of us to read from a book of devotionals. It was funny, such a big guy holding that little book in his mitts; funny also because there was nothing really religious about him. I'd never seen a priest enjoy life, or *understand* it, the way Jack did. He wasn't pious or profound. He was just plugged in.

You could feel it in every corner of that house—the peacefulness, the simple pleasure of stillness. I'd never seen anything quite like it before, how people could just sit and *be* without having to do, say, or act like something. I mean, when one person talked, the other three listened instead of trying to cram a word in edgeways. It was weird. And during those first couple of meals together, I couldn't get used to it. I thought the whole Butterfield clan were a bunch of cold fish. It took me a while to understand that when someone wanted to say something, everyone else was really interested to hear. They were responding instead of reacting. It was then I began to feel, after all those wasted years, what it was like to really be accepted. Not for what I could do or deliver or in any other way conjure up, but just for me. Dion. Period.

And because it was such a strange and new sensation, it frightened me. But it also caught my attention, like a good smell or something bright in the night sky. I was drawn toward Jack, toward what he had, and even when I dug my heels in and tried to turn away, my ears kept hearing and my eyes kept seeing, without any cooperation from me. Some parched part of my soul wanted to live. And Jack, by just being who he was, was coaxing it into being.

He knew the numbers I was running on myself and everyone else. He saw me coming from a long way off and, I guess, he must have recognized something of himself—fourteen years younger, but just as scared and angry—in all the changes I was going through. At least that's the way it seemed to me. Because everything Jack said cut through the confusion, right to the heart of what was wrong. Jack knew what I was going through, but more important, he knew *me*. I may have been a textbook case addict, a potential statistic on some list of born losers, but I was also a person, and it was the person Jack reached out to. For the first time it seemed like someone was talking to me, not at me, and not just wrestling with the shadowy alter egos I threw up like the walls of a maze. It wasn't always easy, and it was never what I was used to hearing, but it was true. And truth has a ring that reaches down right into your spirit.

He talked from the solid foundation of utter simplicity, from the Sermon on the Mount and the assurance of our daily bread. Blessed are the poor in spirit, he told me. Blessed are those who can accept their powerlessness. Live a day at a time. If you pray, why worry? If you worry, why pray?

There is a God, Jack told me. A power higher than ourselves. He answers our prayers. He gives us serenity. Serenity was a word I'd hardly ever heard. No one ever came up to me on the street corner and asked, "Hey, man, how's your serenity?" "Hey, man you look serene." It was always, "Who's got some dynamite stuff?" But it wasn't just that word that was beginning to stir things deep down inside. It was what I saw in him, radiating like warmth itself, beginning to melt the walls of my cave.

All of which, naturally, was making me real uncomfortable. "Who does your old man think he is?" I'd shout at Susan whenever we were by ourselves. "What's he got, a pipeline to God?" But the truth was, what he had I wanted. Even if I didn't know it.

Two weeks after we'd arrived in Miami, Jack got some tragic news. His son, Susan's half-brother, had died of alcoholic convulsions. He was thirty-eight years old. It was then that he did something that made me believe, finally and forever, that Jack was genuine, that it wasn't all just words and notions. He broke down and cried. Jack wept like a baby and you could have knocked me over with a feather. I'd just never seen anything like that

before in my life. I'd always thought humility was humiliation, that brokenness was defeat, that dependency was
death. Yet here was a man—a strong man with authority
and strength—who had tears streaking down his face, un-
ashamed to show what he really felt. Seeing him in that
painful moment of weakness brought it home to me that I
was weak, too—weak as a baby. But in that weakness, in
letting myself feel weak, there was strength. Jack's
strength. I wasn't going to lose precious respect by opening the door to others. I wouldn't lose what I never had
by giving up control. I, too, wanted to feel the tears on
my cheeks. I was tired of being sick and tired.

The next day I went up to Baltimore with him to
claim his son's body. What was being set in motion now
couldn't be stopped. Jack wasn't just teaching me what it
meant to be a real man—a man who intended to love
and be loved—he was showing me from the drama of his
own life. It was a long trip and by the time we finally got
to the hotel, night was falling. We got ready for bed and
just before lights out, Jack did another amazing thing. He
got down on his knees, bowed his head and began to pray
softly. It wasn't some overblown petition to the Almighty.
Instead, it was as if he were talking to an old and trusted
friend and, to me that was the most radical realization of
all. It got to me, even more than seeing a full-grown man,
with plenty to be proud of and an image to uphold, fold-
ing his hands and closing his eyes like a little kid. This
wasn't some ritual an old guy goes through to make himself feel better. This was a man asking—gently, almost
innocently—for strength. There was nothing tentative in
Jack's prayer, nothing half-hearted about the blessing he
asked for his wife, his daughter, his dead son, and me.
He was talking because he knew someone was listening.

He must have seen the look in my eyes, the bewildered expression on my face, because after he was finished he sat on the edge of the bed and, in that same, gentle, nonthreatening tone, he began to tell me about his God. And I listened. For the first time I began to understand that God wasn't someone interested in you only if you could toe the line, follow all the rules, and fill a book with good deeds. He wanted to meet me where I was, Jack said, down there at the end of the rope where I was dangling. I didn't have to prove anything to Him. What could I do for God that He hadn't already done for me? It was time to stop performing, my father-in-law told me, catching and holding my attention with his shining eyes. I could finally climb down off the stage. The show was over.

Put your problems in His hands, Jack urged in the stillness of that rented room, and just then something inside started to crumble like a sand castle at the edge of the sea. Who was I kidding anymore, I asked myself? One of the first things Jack had told me was that he was an alcoholic. But I never saw him take a drink. There I was, drinking and telling myself I wasn't hooked. It didn't make sense. He was admitting what I couldn't—his weakness—and instead of humiliation and shame, it had given him strength and dignity. How could I get what he had, what I needed more than my next breath of air? Where did I go to surrender?

"Pray." That's what Jack suggested. Get on your knees and talk to Him. He's your best friend. He didn't get technical about it. "Ask Him," he said. Whoever I thought He might be. Trust Him.

So I tried it. I got down, copying Jack, and I talked to God. Take it away, I said. Take it all away—the booze

and the pills and all the dark places inside. I was overcome. I couldn't fight another day. Throw me a lifeline,
God, if You're there.

When I was a kid, going to Mount Carmel on a Sunday morning with my dad, we used to hear the bells of
the chapel ringing from blocks away. At the deep, rich
sound of it, he would stop and beat his chest with a fist,
right over the heart. "What's going on?" I asked. And
he'd hold his finger over his lips; "Shhhh . . ." It was only
later I found out that they were ringing the bells at the
moment of consecrating the host, so everyone in the
neighborhood would know that a special time was at
hand.

Something was consecrated that night in a Baltimore
hotel room, April 1st, 1968—a time for a fool's tears if
ever there was one. A reckoning long overdue finally
came around and it was like the strange city surrounding
us stopped for a moment of suspended time, while somewhere, church bells chimed. I bowed my head and bent
my knee and begged for help. I said goodbye to drinking
and drugs and all the devouring needs they fed, forever.
I was three months shy of my twenty-ninth birthday, but
that night I felt like I climbed out of the womb for the
very first time.

CHAPTER 16

Abraham, Martin and John

ANGELS were waiting in the wings. I'd swear it was true. With Jack's help I had reached a turning point in my life and around the corner were blessings I'd never imagined. I think God maybe knew I needed lots of encouragement—and He could hardly wait to start sending good things my way.

In the weeks that followed I hung around Jack as much as I could—as much as he'd let me. Now that I'd had a taste, I wanted to know more about God, more about the spiritual lessons that underscored my father-in-law's life. It was like anything else, he used to say. Take a look around. You can't miss it. If you don't eat and you don't sleep, you wear yourself out. That's physics. Chemistry. There are laws like that for the spirit. And if you break them, the results are just as certain. A self-willed person is full of resentment and fear and always in conflict with others. That's how you know he's violating the principles. It's as simple as that.

It really was. I was finding that out quick. A power much greater than I'd ever be—a power that had first been shown to me that night in Nyack—had just released me from the obsession for drinking and drugs. Such a joy welled up inside when I realized that I was finally free, when I knew this was something I wasn't fixing up on my own. What put a big smile on my face, and tears of gratitude in my eyes, was knowing that God had done this on His own. With no help from me. It was His mercy that released me from that stale captivity, not my frantic scheming. That made all the difference in the world.

The admission that I was an addict, with an addictive personality rooted in an addictive family tree, was playing a whole new tune in my head. I'd been caught up in it for a long time, and Jack didn't mince words when it came to describing how it might have all ended. I'd be dead before my time and against my will, he told me, and to back it up, he talked about his own wrong turn into the valley of shadows. "I was there," he'd say softly and there was no doubt he had been. "For a drunk like me, the verdict was already in. Death, disease, the gutter." That was something they never told me in the psycho ward and it started to open me up. I got honest with myself. I had the freedom to look at who I was for the first time because I'd given up fighting other people. It was hard to believe anymore that if everyone else just straightened out, I'd be fine. It was time to get to work from the inside and my starting point was surrender.

Jack shared with me what I liked to call "the language of the heart." All my life God was someone you thought about on Sunday, if then, and here it would be a Tuesday afternoon and we'd be sitting on the patio, sipping iced tea underneath the palm trees, talking about the Almighty. When it comes right down to it, what happened to me in the spring of 1968 was that I became teachable for the first time. And Jack was the professor. Only it never seemed like he was delivering a lecture or quoting from a textbook. He had a way of talking about those unchanging principles—what spirituality was really all about—in a way that made total sense to me. He wasn't trying to sell me a bundle of beliefs. He wasn't testing out some theological theory. He wasn't shooting off his mouth about all his accomplishments as a man of faith. He was letting me—leading me—into the only kind of knowledge that I understood, the kind that comes from experience.

Jack took the word "blame" out of my vocabulary. Good riddance. Man, I used to love to blame people— and no one more than myself. "You've got to forgive yourself first," Jack would say. "God forgives you and if He does, then you've got no business holding out." God had exclusive rights on who gets pardoned, I realized, and I'd just gotten an eleventh-hour reprieve. The past was finally put behind me. I could start moving forward.

Yet, at the same time, I knew there were things back there that also needed to be put to rest. It would have been easy to just shrug off all the wounds, anger, and confusion I'd left in my trail, chalk it off to another guy named Dion who didn't know what he was doing. But as long as I knew I had the power to do it, I also knew I had to go back—not to soothe my guilt, but just to clean off my side of the ledger.

I started with Susan. I'm not sure she really believed

me when I told her that something basic had changed, that I really was a new man. I'm not sure she was supposed to believe me. To resolve some of the fears and insecurity in her own life, Susan had taken up going to a local church, getting tight with some new girlfriends. They started meeting regularly and for a while I was sure they were talking about Topic A—yours truly. I finally got up the nerve to ask and I'll never forget her answer. "It's for me, Dion," she said. "It's something I'm doing for myself."

I knew I'd have to earn her trust again, but there must have been something sincere in the tone of my voice when I held her hand, looked into her eyes and asked her please to forgive me. I wanted her to tell me everything she was holding against me, to get it out and over with, now and forever. We weren't kidding each other, there was a lot of rebuilding to do, but I knew she was checking me out from that day on, watching and weighing, and that actually felt good. Like a test you know you've got clinched.

Jack was the first man I ever really trusted; maybe the first I ever really let into my life. It was like I had another chance at having a father and—I like to think—he had another chance at having a son. But that didn't mean there weren't bridges I needed to cross again with my real dad. I rang him up and made arrangements to get together back in New York.

During the plane ride north, I took a long, hard look at the part I played in my own past. How had a lifetime of selfishness threatened the love between my folks and me? Was I responsible for the way things went down as much as my mom, my dad, or the two of them together trying to be married, to be parents, and to be happy all at the same time? Just like I expected something of them, maybe they'd expected something of me, some kind of unconditional love and honor that I was too stubborn to give in to. I'd never really accepted them for who they were, warts and all, I thought, as the plane circled the city and dipped down through the smoky sky. It wasn't that I was into beating myself up or anything. I just wanted to take a realistic inventory, because all my life the only things I'd tallied up were the gold stars I'd earned on my own—the applause, the money, the things I did for people to get them to like me. I needed love. Wasn't that something I had in common with Frances and Pasquale?

We had lunch in the neighborhood, my dad and I, sharing some of Joe's good provolone with a couple of bottles of cream soda. I got right to the point. "I've always seen you as a failure, Pop," I confessed, "and I just couldn't deal with everyone putting you down all the time." I don't know whether I expected him to slap me upside the head or burst out crying, but he just sat there chewing his sandwich and listening. I didn't know what else to do but roll on. "I've always had a lot of resentment toward you," I continued. "And I never knew how to express it. How to vent it. So I just shoved it all inside until it turned to bitterness. Can you forgive me for holding so much against you for all that time? Can you believe me when I tell you that I love you, just for who you are? I don't want to change you, Pop. Not anymore."

Another long moment passed before he stood up, carefully finishing off the heel of his bread and downing the last swallow of soda. Only then did he look at me. And smiled. "Are you kidding?" he said. "Forget it. Hey, let's go down to the Botanical Gardens and watch the ducks. You know, D, they don't work; they never worry. God gave them wings to fly and food to eat, and all they do is swim around and quack. We could learn something from them. Know what I mean?" And for the first time, I felt like I did.

I gotta be honest. My dad wasn't the kind of role model he should have been. There was no use pretending he was. But that didn't matter. Not anymore. I wasn't stuck, trying to get him to be my dad, doing what I thought a dad should do. I let it go and let Pasquale Di-Mucci be himself.

And at the same time I found the strength to be who I really was for my mom—to tell her how it felt to constantly be criticized, to be compared to others and found wanting. Back at the height of my popularity, I'd make an appearance on "Ed Sullivan" or something, a star shining in a million living rooms except my own. I'd come home with a swelled head ready to be burst. And my mom was always there to oblige me. "Don't wear blue socks with a gray suit," she'd say. "Don't slouch. Don't swallow your words." It was her way of holding on to me and as long as I let her do it, she had no way of stopping. It was up to me to show her—not out of resentment and anger, but out of love—that her little boy was all grown up, responsible for himself and his actions.

To tell you the truth I amazed myself. I can't say it still didn't sting when I'd hear that nitpicking tone in her voice. But instead of cringing, instead of trying to top myself just to please her, I was able to tell her exactly how I felt. "Don't do that, mom," I'd say. "I wouldn't compare you with anyone. I love you. Don't make me feel like you can't accept me just for who I am." A lot of times I wasn't so sure she was listening, but I'm also not sure that was always so important. The fact that I could tell her, that I could free myself—that was enough.

I guess there comes a point in everyone's life when you separate the men from the boys and put away the toys. Talking—and listening—to my folks helped me come to that point. I realized how many false beliefs I'd picked up as a kid and kept carrying around with me. When my uncles would put down my dad, I took it personally, like they were actually saying those terrible things about me. But I really had no part of it. I wasn't Pasquale . . . I was Dion. I didn't have to carry that weight. "I told your mother," my dad said to me later that day. "I told her that she shouldn't talk to me like that or she'd drive a wedge between me and my son. But," he said, "these things run deep. I just had to live with it, to accept it." There was that word again—accept. It was becoming a theme, recurring in every part of my life. Accept, Jack had told me, and the more you do, the more peace you can lay claim to.

And once I started rolling down that road, I just couldn't stop. I walked through my life again, remembering people I'd wronged and the places I'd done it to them. I started methodically trying to clean up the past—songwriters, producers, musicians—anyone and everyone I'd ever been arrogant, spiteful, or out of line with. It wasn't just saying I was sorry, either. I'd always been able to say I was sorry, to feel guilty about what I'd done without ever knowing how—or ever wanting—to change. This was different. I wasn't into groveling or trying to make it all up to them, get them back into my life or turn them into buddies. I just wanted to say, "Hey, something happened between us one day, between you and me, and I was wrong. I pray you can find it in your heart to forgive me. If there's anything I can ever do for you, just let me know. I owe you one." That was that and I did it as much for me—to feed that growing glow inside that came from doing the right thing, the real thing—as it did for the people who I'd asked forgiveness from.

I wasn't ashamed anymore. I could look the world in the eye without ever having to wonder what it would be like to run into somebody I'd once shafted. To the best of my ability I made amends and if I could have found that orderly whose teeth I'd knocked out at the Institute for Living I would have. Hey, if you're reading this now, these words are for you, too.

I know what you're thinking—at least those of you who're like me. I had a new lease on life and it was all a little too good to be true, right? Sure, I'd never raped or murdered anyone, but that didn't mean I hadn't contributed my fair share of grief to this old globe. Where was the justice in just walking away from the wreckage of my life? Didn't someone have to pay up?

I guess not. All that Jack had done was point me to God and all that God had done was settle my account. I owed it all to Him and it was in the gratitude I felt that the strength came. To live each day, one at a time. To pray and not worry. To stop fixing people and start loving them.

And, just like Jewish people say at Passover, if that was all God had done for me, it would have been enough. I was sick. Now I was well. But that was just the beginning. Along with my marriage, my self-respect, and my family, He was also laying plans to rescue my career. By the end of that momentous month of April 1968, Susan and I had found a perfect house to begin a new life, nestled in the greenery of a suburban Miami neighborhood. Slowly, over the course of days and weeks, our life took on new rhythms and routines. When I wasn't hanging around Jack, soaking up serenity, I was back home, getting as tight with Susan and Tane as they could stand. I think I would have been happy just to sit in the sun forever, surrounded by the safety of my family, but it wasn't meant to work out that way. When you get something wonderful, it's supposed to be spread around, given away. If you don't it'll just get stale and musty.

Which was pretty much what my music was sounding like right about then. I was toying around with trying to put something on wax but it wasn't until Phil Gernhard, a producer for Laurie Records, brought me a song by a writer named Dick Holler, who was looking to get his music recorded, that things started to click, really click, one more time.

Actually, if it had been up to me, "Abraham, Martin and John," would have stayed just a young songwriter's dream. I listened to the simple, shuffle tune a couple of times, but it never did much for me until Midge, my mother-in-law, happened to hear it, and keyed in right away on what it was laying down. "That song is the truth, Dion," she said, and the strength of that conviction brought me back to listen again.

This time I picked up on what had passed me by before. I realized that what these four guys—Lincoln, King, and the Kennedys—had in common was a dream. It was like they had the courage to believe that a state of love really can exist. And they were trying to get others to believe it, too. They wanted to change the world.

Right about then, the world could've used some changing. Vietnam, the riots in Chicago, the assassination of Bobby Kennedy—there was turmoil everywhere.

Wayne Newton and Mac Davis joining me
for some do-wop in Vegas, 1976

With Bruce Springsteen in Manhattan, 1976

On ''The Tonight Show''
with Rob Reiner and
Penny Marshall, 1977

On Cher's show in 1977

At the Bottom Line with
Lou Reed

Roz Levin Perlmutter

Running in a 10K race in
Fort Lauderdale

Al Green and I when we were recording
gospel music together for the TV show
"More Than Music"

Santos

Joan Jett and I backstage at "Late Night
with David Letterman"

Santos

Tony de Fontes

Billy Joel, Paul Simon, Bruce Springsteen, and Lou Reed singing backup for me at Madison Square Garden, 1987. It was a benefit for the N.Y. Children's Health Project to raise money for a mobile medical unit to help homeless children.

Michael J. Friedman

With Darlene Love and Phoebe Snow at Radio City Music Hall, June 1987

Michael J. Friedman

With Little Steven and Paul Shaffer back-stage at Radio City Music Hall, June 1987

Zach Glickman and I at Radio City Music Hall, June 1987

Michael J. Friedman

At Radio City for the WCBS-FM anniversary show: The Wanderer comes home, June 19, 1987.

Tom LaPointe

Me and my girls: Susan, Tane, Lark, and
August, Valentine's Day, 1988

"Abraham, Martin and John" was a way of reminding people that they could aspire to great things, even in the midst of tragedy and confusion. Unlike any other song I'd ever recorded, here was one that might help point people toward the good—the good that may die young but that never gave up being hopeful for tomorrow.

With a young producer named Phil Gernhard, I cut a version of "Abraham, Martin and John," with a soft, lilting arrangement to focus the meaning of the words and highlight a yearning melody. I took it back to the company where I'd started, going on ten years ago, Laurie Records—back to Gene and Bob and Alan. Back to a feeling of doing music just because it's something you love.

There was no big fanfare, no five-year contract for six-figure sums. Like in the old days, we just agreed to let it out, work it a little, and see what happened. By November of that year, "Abraham, Martin and John" had reached number four on the charts. It was my tenth Top Ten single.

CHAPTER 17

Sanctuary

WITH a deep sigh of total relief, all I wanted to do—all I could do—was sit back, smile, and count the blessings, naming them off on the fingers of both hands and the toes of my two feet. Whether I went to the market, stayed home, had roast beef, or had none, I really did feel like a little kid again, eager to learn, happy just to be drawing breath, greeting each morning like I was the guest of honor at a surprise party.

I've heard it said that everyone's locked into a script for their lives, that no matter what kind of moves we make, it's all been figured out beforehand by the Big Plot Hatcher in the Sky. I don't know. Maybe that's all there is to it—we're just actors on a stage, reading lines that were written for us before we were born. But it makes me wonder, what's the third act of my personal drama? I mean, there's something strange, kind of unpredictable, about it all, if you ask me. My story was wrapped up pretty neatly—a tragedy in the grand style, complete with fans and friends laying wreaths around a good-looking corpse in an open casket. But, well, something happened, and the end came full circle back to the beginning: The burnt-out hero turned into a happy-go-lucky kid again, the same boy that had once strolled down 187th Street waving hello to everyone he knew, humming a tune under his breath, playing tag with the sun between the shadows of the tenement houses.

It wasn't supposed to happen that way, was it? By rights, someone else should be writing this book, some hired hack who could sum it all up with the well-chosen phrases you always read in the obituaries. Dion is dead. Long live his music and his memory. R.I.P. But, like some wiseguy said, reports of my death have been greatly exaggerated. Instead I have the distinct pleasure of a happy ending—the ultimate plot twist—where the bad guy ends up the good guy and the corpse turns into a grey haired grandpa, telling tall tales to his children's children, sitting on his knee.

It's the cynic in me—maybe the cynic in you, too—that finds happy endings a little hard to swallow. How does the momentum—that blind head of steam you build up across the years—suddenly start slowing, turning, and taking you in a new direction? Why does the worm turn, the dog have his day, the ugly duckling become the beautiful bird?

Sorry, but I haven't got a clue. I'm no rocket scientist when it comes to figuring out what the Creator's got up His sleeve. All I can tell you is what you've probably already scoped out for yourself: Don't bet on the sure thing. God favors the long shot.

By the time '69 showed itself, like a seedling in the dirt, all kinds of long shots were starting to pay off for me. With "Abraham, Martin and John" I was on top again, only this time with a whole new kind of music. And a whole new reason for singing. I wasn't looking for hit formulas anymore, but don't get me wrong. It still felt great to be driving down the street and catch your song on the airwaves. With that tune especially, the warm glow came from a brand-new perspective. I wasn't out to shower glory on myself anymore. But even more important, I'd busted out of that private world I'd created with music, the way I'd learned to escape all the things I couldn't face or fix.

Instead, I started seeing singing, writing, and playing, as my unique gift from God, meant to be used. I gave up trying to hook an audience with clever put-downs of fast and easy girlfriends. I quit trying to keep on top of the latest trends, the baddest players, and the biggest budgets. But at the same time, what I might have wanted to write off as wasted years were really being redeemed. I'd picked up a lot during my time in the Village, and it all started coming together in the folk flavors of my new stuff. I was trying to say it just with words and melody—me and my guitar—and, with "Abraham, Martin and John" I'd rediscovered my audience, the same ones who'd always been there, clear back to those front-stoop sessions with Mike the stonecutter's tape recorder. They'd grown up, too.

My follow-up was a laid back version of "Purple Haze." It didn't do much, but I still dig the way Hendrix's drug-hazed lyrics can be turned into a love song, complete with a scat-sung bridge. There was more of that kind of easy-flowing music on an album I did for Laurie early that year. I included stuff by Dylan, Joni

Mitchell, and Leonard Cohen, some blues and a couple of originals, with Gernhard helping me pull it all together.

Phil also introduced me to Zach Glickman, a Baltimore boy I took a liking to right away. Neither one of us pushed it, but as we got to know each other, it just seemed right. With Zach, what you saw was what you got—a good businessman, savvy and always a couple of steps ahead. But there was also this soft spot, something vulnerable about the guy, and that's what counted. He was interested in what I wanted to do, not manufacturing idols. I asked him to be my manager.

And what I really wanted to do, musically anyway, was reflect some of the changes that had been coming down for me. Instead of a way out, songs were becoming a diary, a way to try and make sense, and say thanks, for all those changes. And even while I was trying to turn it all into music, it was still unfolding around me. Susan was pregnant again and slowly, but steadily, the bonds of our marriage were being strengthened. I'd never thought of leaving my wife, no matter how bad things got, but I could sure remember times when she might have been better off for it. Wounds, I was beginning to understand, do heal—an everyday miracle I didn't want to take for granted. Suddenly, family was important again, especially after mom and pop decided to pull up stakes and follow us down to the swamps and the surf. We were drawing close, maybe for the first time, maybe closer than ever before.

And when I was out of that circle of family and home, Jack was there, like a lifeline. Off of "Abraham, Martin and John," I'd started getting bookings, mostly colleges, across the country. I was out on the road, but I was still under spiritual construction, a shell-shock victim, basically. The only way I could keep it together was to remember the simple things, like Jack reading his devotional.

"Put your effort into living for today," he'd tell me when I'd call from some hotel room in the middle of the night. "Leave the results to God. Put your life in His hands. Pray each day to understand a little more of His will, then pray again for the strength to do that will. You'll make mistakes. Don't worry about it. Have confidence in God's plan for you." Confidence. I could hear it in his voice. He always said the same thing, and I always hung up hanging on to Jack's simple slogans. They were life to me. And the life I was living—the script with my name on it—was happening in a world that was finally making sense.

Working with Zach and Phil, I also held on to keeping things simple. The hit had turned up the heat again, but instead of jumping back on the bandwagon, I set my own pace, working small clubs and halls and recording only occasionally. I was getting a whole new pleasure out of playing live, at places like the Troubadour in L.A., or the Bitter End in New York. About the biggest I wanted it to get was a gig at Carnegie Hall and that's only because I'd loved the place ever since my grandfather took me there to hear opera as a kid.

Mostly I was working the smaller venues, solo with a guitar. It was almost therapeutic. With just you up there, having to fill those speakers with music, the only thing that goes over is what's real. I started to learn to trust my instincts again, to open up and sing about what I was feeling. I was coming out of isolation, getting lots of encouragement from the audience, and from the artists I was working with. The coffeehouse club scene was thriving, giving regular work to up-and-comers like Bonnie Raitt, Melanie, Seals and Crofts, and Hall and Oates. We all shared bills together at places like the El Mocambo in Toronto, a couple of classy coffeehouses in Philly, and Max's Kansas City in New York. Max's is where I first met some of the new comics, too—guys like Gabe Kaplan and Steve Martin. When I wasn't on the road I'd make local appearances in Miami, sometimes with a hometown favorite named Jimmy Buffett. I was back in the company of some exciting, talented artists, and it felt better than ever before. I'd stopped scrambling, scheming to stay on top. What got me going about music now was the pleasure it was giving others. It was like being the bearer of good news and I dug it.

Late that year, I was asked to be on "The Smothers Brothers Show," along with George Harrison and Donovan. The program had been kicking up a little dust with its hip humor and, for my money, it was my best TV performance, thanks to a musicians' strike that had stripped down the accompaniment to guitar and vocals— exactly what I was doing live on stage. I had no one else to be but myself, and no other way to do it but relax.

The show aired the night we brought home Lark, our second daughter. The coincidence kind of summed it all up: my music, my marriage, my family, my desire— for the first time it was all pulling in the right direction. I had new mouths to feed, new songs to sing, and a new address on my front door. A year ago it would have seemed like somebody else's life, but I wasn't asking any questions. I hung on with both hands.

I hear Einstein was bad at arithmetic and Moses herded sheep for forty years. I've always liked those stories, maybe because I'm a slow learner and I know what it feels like to be in one place for a long time, waiting on God without even knowing it. Along with every other new thing in my life, a new decade had rolled around, and with it, a stretch of time when weeks flowed into months and months into years, all with the same gentle rhythm. The Seventies was like a long convalescence after a bout with some deadly disease. I basked in the Florida sun in the embrace of my family and the unhurried pleasures of my music. I used to mark my life out in anxious hours. Now it stretched out across the lazy days, the settled routine of a happy man.

I was still sailing from the success of "Abraham, Martin and John" when Zach put together a generous recording deal with Warner Brothers Records. Like my manager, Warner Brothers was interested in what *I* wanted to do, and the family feeling that the staff shared with the artists made it all that much more relaxed. The titles of my first three albums for the label tell the whole story—*Sit Down Old Friend, You're Not Alone, Sanctuary*. It was the music of a mellow Indian summer, soft and balmy, sometimes wistful, sometimes buoyant.

I was still writing a diary, I guess, putting it all down in tunes like "Your Own Backyard," being as honest as I could about what had happened to me—the drugs, the delusions and the decisions that turned it all around. I was still singing the blues—once you get that in your blood, it never lets you go—and still picking up tunes from some of the best young songwriters on the scene; guys like Tony Fasce and Bill Tuohy who had a knack of putting just what I was thinking into thoughtful lyrics. Gernhard was on board as producer, Zach was behind the scenes. The people who'd gathered around me were part of another kind of family and we shared the trust and love and honesty that goes with that bond.

Once I was really able to slow down and savor it, I realized I got a lot of simple joy out of my profession. But even while I was just kicking back, letting the songs spell out the peace I felt in my heart, I was still learning, sharpening the craft, fine-tuning the fine art of communicating. In the old days all I ever did on stage was my hits. I'd jump out from the wings, throw open my arms, and let the little girls go crazy. It was different now. I had to care about the people, acknowledge who they were and where I wanted to take them, and the more I could reach out beyond the bright lights, the more it was like me just talking to them, one on one, and the more faith I had that this was all part of the plan. God was showing me how to use His gifts to do some good. Even in my worst days, He had never taken the talent for music away from me. He doesn't work that way. It was another lesson in patience, one more way He taught me the rule of love that had come to govern my life.

In '72 we put together a one-time-only Dion and the Belmonts reunion at Madison Square Garden. No rehearsals, no nothing, just me, the guys, the old songs, and a house packed with fans who wouldn't let us do anything wrong. Freddie might hit a bad note, I might stumble over those musty lyrics, but for them, it didn't matter. We were still four parts of the same whole and together we made up a memory that was precious and true. "Brooklyn Loves Dion" read a huge banner strung across the cheap seats. It's the closest thing I've ever felt to unconditional love, standing on that stage.

By '75 I'd stood on a lot of different stages and sung to a lot of different crowds. Not so different from the old days, maybe, but this time I wasn't splitting my time between standards for the blue hairs and rock for the kids. It was just me, take it or leave it. Whether it was a rock festival in England, a smoky club in Boston or Chicago, out in Vegas as part of a Dick Clark package, on TV with Sonny and Cher, or just sitting around the living room scatting nursery rhymes to the kids, I knew I'd never again have to sing for respect, approval, or someone else's good opinion. It wasn't like that anymore. And it wasn't ever gonna be again.

I put together a couple more albums, including a concept thing called *Suite for Late Summer* that picked up one more time on what had become my favorite themes—gratitude, safe harbor, and second chances. None of the stuff was streaking to the top of the heap, but, if I even noticed, I sure didn't care. Hits, and the hot flash that comes with them, are over almost faster than they happen. I'd found a niche, comfortable as an old shirt, and, if I had my way, that's where I was going to stay.

That left Zach and the folks at Warner Brothers— bless their hearts—to keep the ball rolling. The company had recently signed the legendary Phil Spector to a platinum plated production deal, giving him his own label and free rein to work with any artist on the roster. He chose me—lucky me. They flew me out to Los Angeles and I

drove out to Spector's sprawling mansion in the Hollywood Hills to talk about making the musical masterpiece
that would hitch my wagon to his star.

I hadn't seen the guy since his Teddy Bear days
and, even with all the stories about his fabulous eccen-
tricity floating around, I still wasn't prepared for the
weird scene waiting behind his oak carved front door. On
that first meeting, he pointed directly at me and said,
"Only you know what you have been through. Only you
know where you have been to. There's better things
you're gonna get into. And I'm gonna be there, too." The
house was almost pitch dark as he led me to his den,
humming the chorus of the tune he had written for me.
The only light in the whole place seemed to be this little
five-watt job over the pool table, and Spector kept flitting
in and out of the shadows, talking a mile a minute. And
right in the middle of this ramble, the phone rings. It's
the hospital with news that Phil's trusted bodyguard has
just had a heart attack.

Don't ask me how, but the next thing I knew I was in
the car with him and he was holding a paper bag full of
cash. We tear off to the hospital and I can hardly keep up
with him as he barges into the lobby shouting at the top
of his lungs. He wants immediate attention for his em-
ployee, the best money can buy, and to prove it he
dumps all this cash—big bundles of bills—out of the paper bag and onto the counter. "I speak seven languages,"
he's shouting as they try to figure out who this guy is and
what he's raving about. "I work in this hospital in my
spare time." It was like I was instantly thrown back into
the mad whirlwind that always seems to be blowing up
there around the peaks of superstardom. It made me

happy I was just a humble troubadour, providing for my little family with my trusty guitar. I'd definitely gotten a little old for this kind of craziness.

But I hadn't seen anything yet. The next month we went to the studio to start work on the album. It's like he'd called the union and asked them to send out every off-duty studio cat in town. There were ten guitar players, as many backing singers, two drummers, two bass players, two vibists, and even more people in the control booth. Warner Brothers' president, Joe Smith, was only one of the special guests that dropped in. Cher was there, looking beautiful and willing to play tambourine on something. Little Steven, member of the E Street Band, came by with Bruce Springsteen. I'd known Steve since he played guitar for me back in Vegas, but it was the first time I'd ever met Bruce. He loved the Spector sound and just enjoyed being close to that magic. The Boss was pretty tolerant of Spector's behavior that night. Phil was a little threatened, I think by the Springsteen cover story in *Time* that had come out that week.

Working with Phil Spector could be exciting, frustrating, even a little sad at times. He's a real artist and one who liked to surround himself with spectacle, but it seemed to me he was afraid of failure. He's got the image of a genius and that puts a lot of pressure on himself, always trying to outdo his last masterpiece.

The circus in the studio went on for weeks as we slogged through the album and, for all the energy we put into it, it's a shame none of it ended up in the grooves. Produced and directed by Phil Spector, *Born to Be With You* sounded to most people like a dirge, despite some pretty good material from me, Gerry Goffin, and even

Phil himself. In the end, Spector only had it released in England. I just walked away, happy to be in one piece.

Ten years in the blink of an eye? It seems that way to me now—faces, places, friends, and family. I was learning what's precious and what lasts and I carried those lessons around with me like a spare set of strings for my guitar. It all came so easy, so natural, in cycles of birth and death. Jack passed away and left a hole in my life that I might have fallen into if he hadn't taught me how to take my stand. August, a third little girl, was born and somehow we got the feeling of completeness—that the last member of the DiMucci clan had arrived. Shows and sessions and songs, they came and went. But, behind it all, God was getting ready to hand over one more blessing. Just like Him to save the best for last.

CHAPTER 18

Only a Man

DECEMBER 14,

1979: I was five months into forty years old—devoted father, loving husband, good citizen, the whole bit. The years had rolled up on me and I was running closer now to middle age, that time when you're supposed to kiss off the dreams you had as a kid and say hello to who you really are—to accept the good with the bad. It's not gonna change. No change—kind of scary when you think about it. No wonder you can have a crisis.

I guess I was having my mid-life thing, feeling the changes first in the muscle and bones I'd put through so much over the years. Which is why I got into running. To get in shape for the six-mile races I'd do in Miami when I wasn't on the road, I used to jog every morning through the neighborhood, getting up early and following a little sand and coral road through a pine forest, up and down some low rolling hills. The solitude and single purpose you get with running are things you only know about by doing it yourself, and like every other runner, I used the time to sort things through—figuring, praying.

That hazy winter morning, something was weighing on me, something that kept me from hearing the birds singing in the trees or the distant sound of the suburbs waking up. So much had come together for me, a salvation I'd spent ten years celebrating. Why was I getting the feeling that things were sliding out of focus again? I'd recently put together Streetheart, a great new band, and we were set to promote a new album when Columbia changed presidents and we got lost in the shuffle. The project fell through and the group went its different ways. I was left with this restless itch to *say* something to people through my songs. Only, I was beginning to realize, I didn't know what I wanted to tell them anymore. Singing and writing were a gas, but the songs were also kind of disappearing into thin air. My diary was becoming a monologue.

But that wasn't what was stirring deeply that Friday morning. I had my mind on other things—hearing strange, long forgotten voices and feeling old, familiar temptations.

Don't get me wrong. It wasn't that I would have cheated on Susan. At least, that's what I liked to think. But it was exciting. No denying that. When a twenty-year-old girl, good-looking, fun-loving, lets you know she's interested, you'd have to be dead not to feel the thrill. But you'd have to be a fool to pick up on it. I knew that. So why was I trying to find a loophole, some way to justify what I was feeling? Conflict—some struggle inside—was rising like a bad taste in the back of my throat and with it, the stirring of insecurity, and the pang of need. "Let's get away for the weekend," the girl had said, after I'd let her know I was hip to what was going on between us. "Nothing serious. We don't have to do anything, just enjoy it." I could hear her voice in the back of my brain as my legs automatically kept the pace. There was no way I was going to follow through, and yet. And yet.

It had become kind of a habit by that time, praying my way through the tough spots. But that morning it was more of a sigh than a prayer. I felt cut loose from my mooring, adrift in a mix of emotions. Even as I opened my mouth to say the words, some other part of me was asking a question that I wasn't letting myself hear: "Who's up there listening?"

All I could manage was, "God, it would be nice to be closer to you." Before the words were out of my mouth a tremendous white light broke all around me, radiating out from my chest and streaming through every pore. I kept running, but it seemed like I was on air. It was a light so sudden, so brilliant, so profound that it just washed away everything that stood between me and it. I was bathing in the glow of a thousand candles, a million suns, a galaxy of stars.

But there's more. I saw a figure, a man, in front of me, like He'd been waiting for me, His arms outstretched. And I heard Him speak, words of truth, not in my ear, but in my heart. "I love you," He said. "Don't you know that? I'm your friend. I laid down My life for you. I'm here for you now." I looked behind me, just for a second, because the feeling was that strong—that I'd dropped something, shed an old skin—and when I looked, a ripple deep and wide began to spread out from inside me.

The thing about revelation, the way you know it's real, is when your life is changed. I'd heard in the church that Christ died for my sins, but what I'd never heard was that there wasn't any sin too big for Him to forgive. That nothing we can say or do, no place we can hide will separate us from His love. We've got the choice, but He never changes. God's mind is already made up. He's locked into a total commitment. To me. To you. To everyone He created in His image.

People say to me, "D, tell us about your hot flash on the jogging path." I could take them there, stand them on the spot and point to the place where I saw Christ waiting for me. Not that it would help. It's the kind of thing you either accept or you don't. I know nothing I can say is gonna *make* you believe that a guy can wake up one morning and step right through the gates that divide ignorance from knowledge and life from death. Not if you don't want to.

Yeah, I'd been saved. Maybe it was because my heart was willing, and that the ten years I spent clean and sober had prepared me for that twinkling of an eye. Or maybe it's just because, when you gotta go, you gotta go. I didn't know that in the Bible it says He'll answer your prayer before you can finish speaking it out. I'd never heard the parable of the prodigal son. But none of that really mattered right then. Whether I was ready or not, Jesus called me. What could I do? I said yes.

Understanding would come later, after I'd had a chance to get used to total acceptance from heaven above. Hey, it's not easy. Sure, I'd kicked junk and booze. I'd disconnected the applause meter that had been hooked to my soul. I'd made the best peace I could with the world and the people I loved. So why did I feel such a great release that morning, like a yoke broken off my back? Being good, staying straight and faithful, was just one more round on the performance trip I'd been on my whole life. There was a kind of arrogance, a subtle pride of achievement, that melted away in the warmth of that low-slung December sun. It was like all of Jack's words began to breathe in my mind with new meaning.

He was a sly fox, old Jack. He must have known I'd never have accepted a God personal to just me as part of my recovery. Jesus for me was a plaster figure nailed high on the altar of a dusky church. So Jack could only tell me so much . . . just enough to get my attention. The rest of the story would have to come from Jesus. I loved the truth I heard from Jack, and when he blessed me and sent me out to find that truth in my own life, I fell in love with searching, too. I was conjuring up meaning for my-self, looking for the connection and all the time still feel-ing like the outsider, somewhere deep inside. Jack could only take me so far. Christ had to carry me the rest of the way.

He did it for love. My greed for respect—the lean wolf that stalked my whole life—whimpered and died in the light of Jesus, in His total acceptance of Dion. Accep-tance was the lesson Jack had taught me: to live new every day, accepting what I couldn't control, accepting myself. But rest doesn't come easy when you've grown up in the streets. When that's where you've learned what it means to be a man.

Because that's where my story ends. Back at the be-ginning. It's funny when you think about it. God used the doubts I had about my manhood to show me what man-hood really was. Don't kid yourself. A lot of people who hear my story can relate. There's nothing special about me or about the way I was taught to grow from boy to man. You know the shuffle—learning to hide your feelings, to prove who you are by being something you're not, the code with all its images and icons of macho. Of all the lives lived for better or worse on 187th Street and Crotona Avenue, mine was no different. Gangs, drugs, success itself warped my idea of what being a man was all about. And no one else seemed to know either—no one until Jack, who climbed down into the trenches with me, who would have died for me, I think, to prove that love is real. That kind of man, if you let him, will lead you to another kind of man, the one I met on the jogging path. Whatever else I saw that day—a spirit, a vision, a visitation—I was also seeing a man.

It comes down to this: The most courageous thing a man can do is open his heart to God. And if the courage isn't there, God'll give that in His time, too. There's a prayer I wanted to pray—seeking to comfort instead of being comforted, understanding rather than to be understood, loving rather than to be loved. That's a tall order for most of us, but it's what being strong and wise is all about. Being a servant. I prayed for God's will to be done every day for ten years. That day I understood that His will was for me to love Jesus.

It was only after I burst in with the announcement that Jesus was real that I realized I wasn't telling Susan anything she hadn't known—for years, as it turned out. But she wasn't the only person who'd been quietly praying for me over the long haul. There was my Aunt Loretta, I discovered, who had held me up to the Lord from the time I was a wild, willful kid, roaming the streets. And at the same time I was beginning to see the threads of God's love running back into my past, all sorts of patient, loving Christian folks started turning up in my present. Pat Boone, who I'd worked with in Vegas, happened by at just the right time. Back in my rock 'n' roll days I'd always thought Pat was kind of a goof. Now I wanted to be just as goofy. My next door neighbor turned out to be a Baptist music minister, a good guy who didn't mind passing a lazy afternoon over the fence, talking about the Lord. I read the Bible from cover to cover. Then I read it again, fitting it all together with the Man I'd met on the road that day.

I was looking for any way I could to let people in on what I'd discovered and, naturally, songs started leaking out everywhere. I had a passion to write music that would let people know what value they had. Ever since I heard Hank Williams's voice warbling on the radio, I'd known that a song can reach right around the walls and get to the heart of the matter. Now, after winging it for so long, I finally had a message that matched the joy I got from singing. Let me put you wise—God loves you.

That's the pearl of great price, the hidden treasure at the end of the rainbow. And I wanted to share it. I got it for free. I can't give a much deeper discount than that. I write a song these days, release an album, do a concert, and I don't have to worry about feeling important to feel good. I'm not performing to dazzle the masses anymore. The songs I want to sing are about encouragement, joy, and the peace that flows like a river to the sea. I can't preach, but I can tell a story. And it seems to help when you know the story's true.

There's truth in the songs, even in the old ones. Truth about a kid growing up Italian in America. Truth about the pains and pleasures that almost destroyed him. And truth about the love that saved him. Would I change the story, write some new songs, or sing with a different voice? Not a chance. I was sick, almost dead, but it was the sickness that drove me to my knees and into a new reality. If it all had happened differently somehow, I might never have come into the light at the end of that road on a December morning a lifetime ago.